D1001648

Tiki Barber

FOOTBALL SUPERSTARS

Tiki Barber

Tom Brady

John Elway

Brett Favre

Peyton Manning

Dan Marino

Donovan McNabb

Joe Montana

Walter Payton

Jerry Rice

Ben Roethlisberger

Barry Sanders

FOOTBALL SUPERSTARS

Tiki Barber

David Aretha

CHELSEA HOUSE
PUBLISHERS
An imprint of Infobase Publishing

TIKI BARBER

Copyright © 2008 by Infobase Publishing

Chelsea House
An imprint of Infobase Publishing
132 West 31st Street
New York NY 10001

Library of Congress Cataloging-in-Publication Data

Aretha, David.
  Tiki Barber / David A. Aretha.
     p. cm. -- (Football superstars)
  Includes bibliographical references and index.
  ISBN 978-0-7910-9836-3 (hardcover)
  1. Barber, Tiki, 1975---Juvenile literature. 2. Football players--United States--Biography--Juvenile literature. I. Title. II. Series.

  GV939.B37A74 2008
  796.332092--dc22
  [B]

                              2008007064

Text design by Erik Lindstrom
Cover design by Ben Peterson

Printed in the United States of America

Bang EJB 10 9 8 7 6 5 4 3 2 1

This book is printed on acid-free paper.

All links and Web addresses were checked and verified to be correct at the time of publication. Because of the dynamic nature of the Web, some addresses and links may have changed since publication and may no longer be valid.

CONTENTS

The Cold, Hard Climb

They were words that changed Tiki Barber's life. "Hey, Teek, do you want to come train with me?"

Barber, a struggling **running back** with the New York Giants, was talking on the phone to his teammate Greg Comella. Barber had just finished his second season (1998) in the National Football League. He had **rushed** for just 166 **yards**, averaging a puny 3.2 yards per **carry**. He had been hurt a lot, taking abuse from the massive, powerful "bullies" of pro football.

Barber did not know how to respond to his friend's invitation. A **fullback** built like a tank, Comella was known for his fanatical training regimens. Barber knew that they would be doing more than just jumping jacks. In fact, Comella told him, they would run to the top of a gargantuan hill called

Ramapo off Route 17 in New Jersey. Moreover, it was the dead of winter.

Barber was not the type who shied away from challenges. In fact, he thrived on them. After doctors told him he would never play organized sports, he overcame all odds to make the NFL. When people pigeonholed him as a "jock" back in high school, he bore down and became a straight-A student. Naturally driven, Barber burned to be more than a mediocre NFL player.

"All right, I'll go," he told Comella, as he recalled in his memoir, *Tiki: My Life in the Game and Beyond.* "What time are you leaving?"

"I get up by 5:30, and I'm out of here by 6," Comella said.

For a moment, Barber began to reconsider.

"You're kidding me, right?" Barber said.

"Tiki, c'mon, dude," Comella replied.

During the previous season, Comella and Barber had formed a special relationship. Barber had appreciated how his fullback cleared out 300-pound linemen so that Barber could run to glory. Moreover, each had graduated from a prestigious university—Comella from Stanford, Barber from Virginia—and matched each other intellectually.

BUILDING MORE THAN MUSCLE

The morning after the invitation, Comella drove Barber across the George Washington Bridge, which leads from New York City to New Jersey. Near the township of Mahwah, they entered the Ramapo Valley County Reservation. On a frigid, predawn February morning, Barber stared up at a mammoth, forested incline. Barber and his buddy had the benefit of a trail, but that trail was covered in ice.

"It was a brutal hill," Barber recalled in an address to students at the University of Virginia in 2004. "It was two-and-a-half miles uphill. It was rocky terrain. We'd go out there in late February when it's three degrees outside and there's snow on

Tiki Barber *(left)* and Greg Comella of the New York Giants joke around while stretching during a practice before Super Bowl XXXV in Tampa, Florida. A few years before, in early 1999, Comella invited Barber to run with him in the dead of winter. Those regular training runs, a brutal two-and-a-half miles uphill, helped to turn around Barber's career.

the ground and it's dark and there's no reason to be there other than to push ourselves."

That they did. Over the next two months, Barber and Comella routinely ran up that monstrous hill. Amid the dark solitude, the only sounds they heard were the huff of their breath and the crunch beneath their feet. The two men strengthened more than just their muscles and stamina. They became stronger mentally, and they steeled their conviction.

"I developed my 'why' then," Barber told the Virginia students. "My 'why' was I don't want to be average. I want to be better than average. I tell myself as I'm running this hill the reason I'm doing this is because no one else is doing it. And over those long, long mornings, I developed a passion for what I do."

Barber could have slept in on those cold winter mornings, snug beneath his warm covers. Had he done so, though, he might have become lost in obscurity. The careers of most NFL running backs last only a few years, and the injury-prone, marginally productive Barber could have easily slipped out of the league. But he ripped himself out of bed each morning and embraced his challenge. He was determined to be the best he could be.

In 1999, the following season, his torturous training paid off. Barber upped his rushing average to a solid 4.2 yards per carry, and he caught 66 passes for an impressive 609 yards. A year later, he broke through in grand fashion, rushing for 1,006 yards and leading the Giants to the Super Bowl.

CHALLENGE AFTER CHALLENGE

In subsequent years, Barber pushed himself to even greater heights. He altered his running style and strength-trained with the strongest man in New Jersey. Moreover, he told the *Sporting News* that he learned to "play above the X's and O's." Eventually, he became a perennial Pro Bowler, a Giants record-breaker, and one of the most productive backs in the history of the NFL.

Articulate and charismatic, Barber was more than a football star. He became a media darling and a nationwide sensation. He appeared regularly on talk shows (including his own radio program) and in TV commercials—pitching products from McDonald's to Cadillac. He served as a spokesman for numerous charities, and he talked politics with world leaders.

In the regular-season finale in 2006, Barber rushed for more than 200 yards. And then he left the game. Like Barry Sanders, Sandy Koufax, and very few other athletes, Barber retired at the peak of his career. Having mastered his craft, he sought new challenges—as a sports analyst, author, and TV news journalist.

Just days after retiring from the NFL, Barber signed with NBC to fulfill one of his lifelong dreams: to work as a reporter on the *Today* show. NBC Universal CEO Jeff Zucker welcomed him with open arms. "He's incredibly handsome, he's incredibly

After retiring from the NFL at the peak of his career, Tiki Barber moved on to his next challenge. He fulfilled another of his dreams by joining the *Today* show as a national correspondent in 2007.

charming, he's incredibly personable, and he's incredibly smart," Zucker said at the press conference to announce Barber's signing.

Zucker's words undoubtedly made Geraldine Barber-Hale swell with pride. Thirty-two years earlier, she had given birth to two premature twins, Tiki and Ronde. Both spent their first three days in incubators, and each suffered repeated seizures as little boys. Both were told they would never play competitive sports, and the pair grew up without a father. Yet thanks to Geraldine's love and dedication—and each twin's extraordinary determination—they both achieved incredible success.

This is the story of an NFL great, but it is also the story of his mother and his brother, his friends and his coaches, his wife and his sons. Each of these special people helped make Tiki Barber the superstar he is today.

Growing Up
with Ronde

Looking back, it seems ironic that Tiki and his brother, Ronde, were born in Blacksburg, Virginia. That college town is home to Virginia Tech, where their father had starred as a running back before abandoning his family when the twins were toddlers. Virginia Tech is also the rival school of the University of Virginia, where Tiki and Ronde would star in football. Moreover, when Tiki fulfilled his dream and joined the *Today* show in 2007, his first news assignment was to cover the tragic shooting spree on the Virginia Tech campus.

James "J.B." Barber and Geraldine Barber-Hale had both attended Virginia Tech, and on April 7, 1975, Geraldine gave birth three weeks before her due date. Jamael Orondé entered the world first, his name meaning "firstborn son" in Swahili.

The second baby cried and kicked and fussed so much that his mother named him Atiim Kiambu—"fiery-tempered king."

Their opponents on the gridiron would never believe it, but Ronde and Tiki weighed just four-and-a-half pounds each at birth. As they spent their first three days in incubators, their pediatrician doubted that they would enjoy healthy child-hoods. The doctor even said that they likely would never play contact sports.

Raising a baby is hard enough, but Geraldine (or Gerry) had to work outside the home while raising twins with health problems. For Tiki and Ronde, a fever sometimes caused them to suffer seizures. One day, both boys went into seizure, ter-rifying their helpless mother. Fortunately, the seizures ended once they turned five—a year after their father permanently left the family.

In the early 1970s, J.B. Barber had been a star running back for Virginia Tech. Passed over by the NFL, he tried to make it in the fledgling World Football League (WFL). But J.B. never played a down, and the league folded in 1975 after two seasons of play.

For virtually all of her sons' childhood, Gerry served as two parents in one. Tiki has called her the hardest-working person he has ever seen—NFL players included. The daughter of an Army major (who was killed in the Vietnam War), Gerry worked three jobs to provide for her boys. On weekdays, she held down a full-time job as the director of financial aid and administration for the regional Girl Scout Council. In the eve-nings, she spent up to six hours doing clerical work for insur-ance companies and financial-service firms. On weekends, she worked part time at a birding store.

"As we began to get older," Tiki told *Sports Illustrated*, "we realized how hard it was on my mom to have provided for us. We never wanted for anything. My mom sacrificed her entire life."

Ronde, in *The Virginian-Pilot*, described his mother as "always excitable, always happy." Gerry stressed the values of education and personal responsibility. She also wanted her sons to expand their horizons, even if they could not afford to travel much.

"It was important to me that the boys see different cultures, different ways of life," she told *Sports Illustrated*. "I would take them visiting different people—Asians, African Americans, whites. They would visit different churches. Education is absorbing a little piece of everybody with whom you've come into contact."

Tiki respected his mother immensely, but it pained him to see her go off to work so much. "I remember evenings when my mother would feed us dinner, carefully oversee our homework, and then tuck us into bed," he wrote in his memoir. "I'd hear the door open and close as she left for her third job of the day. We would lie there and cry out of sheer loneliness."

A SHY BOY IN ROANOKE

In his book, Barber describes himself as shy as a child. He and his family lived northeast of Blacksburg in Roanoke, Virginia. The twins did not venture much out of their city, but they did like to cruise the streets on their bicycles.

Feeling ambitious one day, Tiki and Ronde peddled at least four miles uphill—out of Roanoke Valley and into the surrounding hills. Odd as it may seem, they went to knock on the door of Debbie Reynolds, a movie star from the 1950s and '60s. Reynolds is also the mother of Carrie Fisher—Princess Leia in *Star Wars*. The twins' love of that movie inspired their daring venture.

Though no one answered the door at Reynolds's home, the journey inspired Tiki. As he stood high in the hills, he stared in awe at the endless view below. For the first time, he realized that a great big world was out there—one he lusted to explore.

Tiki excelled at sports as a child, but another bike excursion nearly ended his athletic dreams. While riding in a construction site at age 12, he accidentally tumbled down

The Barber brothers were foes only when their teams squared off in the NFL. Here, Tiki and Ronde Barber meet up after the New York Giants defeated the Tampa Bay Buccaneers 14-3 on October 29, 2006. While growing up, they were seemingly inseparable. "We always had each other—to hang out with, do homework, share life," Ronde said.

a 30-foot (9-meter) excavation hole. He severely damaged his knee, prompting a doctor to pronounce that he would never play sports again. Like Tiki's pediatrician, the doctor underestimated the young man's desire. Soon he was back on the sporting fields, stronger than ever.

While taking part in a wrestling match in junior high school, Tiki endured one of the most painful moments of his adolescence. This time, the pain was emotional. His father, who had not seen his children in a decade, showed up at their match. He called out to Tiki and Ronde, but he did not know which was which.

The twins responded coldly, but inside, Tiki wrote, "My gut churned. Hurt, pride, longing, fear, indifference, confusion, and anger, lots of anger—everything mixed up inside me."

J.B. again disappeared from his sons' lives, and the twins went on with theirs. Tiki and Ronde attended Roanoke's Cave Spring High School, where they found their calling on the football field and blossomed as young men.

BUSTING OUT OF THE BOX

The student population at Cave Spring High School was, according to Tiki's estimate, 95 percent white. A generation earlier, a black student would have likely felt threatened in a white-dominated school. In Prince Edward County, Virginia, not far from Roanoke, local white officials shut down their public schools from 1959 to 1964 because they did not want white students mixing with black students. (Whites built a private academy exclusively for white students.)

But at Cave Spring in the early 1990s, the Barber twins did not feel out of place. Tiki has insisted that he never felt threatened or discriminated against in his four years of high school. Both brothers were low-key and straight-laced, especially Tiki. He never smoke or drank. Instead of partying with the Cave Spring crazies, he hung out at his girlfriend Robin's house. Sometimes Ronde and *his* girlfriend—and maybe another friend—would go to Robin's house, too, and they would talk or watch movies. The only time Tiki "walked on the wild side" was when he drank a wine cooler as a high school senior. Robin got so mad at Tiki that she refused to speak to him for two hours.

Tiki has credited his mother, his brother, and Robin for keeping him on the straight and narrow. He may have been a "geek," as he has often said, but his priorities were certainly in order. He paid attention in school and put great effort into his homework. The more people praised his athletic feats, the more determined he became to excel in the classroom. He did not want to be typecast as just an "athlete."

Perhaps race played a part of it. For decades, many African-American men have been lauded for their athleticism at the exclusion of their other qualities. Until the 1980s, in fact, many people did not think that African Americans would make good **quarterbacks** because they "weren't smart enough." (Given the opportunity, many African Americans went on to become great quarterbacks.) Tiki did not want people to think that he excelled because he was born with talent. He worked extremely hard to hone his football skills, he felt, and on top of that, he was more than just a football player—much more.

"Don't put me in a box," Barber wrote in his memoir. "Don't do it, because I will make it my goal to bust out of that box. Then I'll dismantle it, put it back together as a soapbox, climb on top of it, and tell you that you're wrong to put people in boxes."

Tiki studied so hard at Cave Spring that he graduated with a 4.0 grade-point average. He participated in the Olympics of the Mind, a competition that stressed creative problem-solving. In the spring of 1993, he graduated high school as a valedictorian.

Yet no matter how well he excelled academically, the community knew Tiki as a football phenom. In his memoir, Barber recalls in detail a single play that captured his joy for the game. As a junior, he took a **handoff** and bolted 40 yards for a **touchdown**, leaving one defender after the other in the dust.

Tiki was elated—not because of the cheers and adulation, but because he had accomplished something special. For

Barber, storming down the field while breaking **tackle** after tackle made him feel like a million bucks. He couldn't wait for his next carry.

ALL-EVERYTHING

In high school, Ronde excelled on defense while his brother starred at running back. Steve Spangler, their football coach in middle school and high school, said it was "fun to coach" the dynamic duo. "If there was a problem—say, Tiki was fumbling—you didn't have to say anything to Tiki, because Ronde took care of it," Spangler told *Sports Illustrated.* "They are each other's conscience."

Blazingly fast—as well as quick and shifty—Tiki was almost impossible to stop one on one. Even before the big 40-yard run that he fondly recalled, Tiki caught people's attention. As a sophomore, he was named the Roanoke Valley Offensive Player of the Year. He also earned *Roanoke Times* All-District kudos as a sophomore for the first of three straight seasons.

The honors only got bigger during his junior and senior campaigns. In both years, he was named All-Region and Male Athlete of the Year. As a senior, he served as a co-captain of the Cave Spring Knights and earned All-American honors from the Super Prep recruiting service. His production was staggering: On 567 career carries, he ran for 3,628 yards (6.4 per rush) and 41 touchdowns.

Each spring, Tiki also excelled in track. Twice he won the state indoor and outdoor long-jump titles. He also took the state title in the triple jump as a senior. His most impressive feat came in the national high school finals of the long jump in 1992. He finished second.

The Knight Award was presented to the Cave Spring student who best excelled in academics, athletics, and extra-curricular activities. In 1993, Tiki was, of course, the hands-down winner.

UVA HITS THE JACKPOT

As their senior season got underway, Tiki and Ronde had to decide where to go to college. Although they had been on an airplane only once in their lives, they were ready to expand their horizons.

Ronde and Tiki were flooded with football scholarship offers. At first, all they knew was that they would go to the same school. Mom had hoped that school would be Virginia

BROTHERS AND PALS

When Tiki and Ronde Barber were little, they sometimes wore their father's old Virginia Tech jerseys to bed. But Dad was no longer part of their lives, and Mom left for work in the evenings. For much of their boyhoods, all Tiki and Ronde had were each other.

"We have always been good friends, as well as brothers, and we have done everything together," Ronde told *The Virginian-Pilot*.

Physically, the identical twins are just that—at least from the neck up. Ronde's face has a slightly more rugged look, but it's barely perceptible. He even shares Tiki's beaming smile, and each boasts a glistening set of ultra-white teeth.

As kids, Tiki and Ronde seemingly did everything together: schoolwork, riding bikes, and just hanging out. In junior high school, the twins joined the wrestling team, with Tiki competing in the 134-pound class. Because they did not want to compete against each other, Ronde lost eight pounds so that he could wrestle with the 126-pounders.

Tiki pulled better grades in high school, but Ronde was no slouch either, logging a 3.3 grade-point average. In college,

Tech, her alma mater and the closest major school to Roanoke. To the twins, though, Virginia Tech was *too* close to home, and they did not want to follow in their father's footsteps.

Eventually, they narrowed their list down to five schools: Clemson, Michigan, UCLA, Penn State, and Virginia. However, they quickly knocked four of those off the list. They visited Clemson but were turned off by how athletes received the "royal treatment"—such as having their own dining room.

they shared a suite and majored in the same subject: business. Though both were shy as youngsters, Ronde could be a little more devilish. During a high school homecoming parade, he dressed in Knight body armor and pretended he was Tiki.

It would not be the last time that Ronde exploited his brother's identity. On *Late Night with Conan O'Brien* in September 2007, Tiki revealed a couple of doozies. On the night before the Giants played in the NFC Championship Game in January 2001, Ronde partied into the wee hours while telling strangers he was Tiki. They went home wondering why the Giants' star player was not in bed getting his needed rest. On another occasion, Ronde walked through the streets of New York wearing a replica Tiki Barber Giants jersey. Pedestrians thought that Tiki was on an ego trip!

Mostly, though, the brothers have been the best of companions. "Even if there was nobody else," Ronde said in *Sports Illustrated*, "we always had each other—to hang out with, do homework, share life." Echoed Tiki: "I knew there would always be one person who would never be a bad guy to me. It really makes a difference."

Although Geraldine Barber-Hale had hoped her sons would go to Virginia Tech—her alma mater—Tiki and Ronde Barber decided to attend the University of Virginia. Here, Tiki *(right)* and Ronde escort their mother before a 1996 game against Clemson at Scott Stadium in Charlottesville, Virginia.

Michigan, Tiki feared, possessed too strong of a football program. He sensed that the Wolverines would move him to another position or designate him to special teams. Also, when the recruiter from Michigan had to cancel his visit because of a snowstorm, they realized that the North might be a little too chilly for their taste.

UCLA seemed glamorous, but the Barbers never visited that school or Penn State. The University of Virginia, they soon discovered, was just right for them. UVA, founded by President

Thomas Jefferson in 1819, ranked as the premier school in the state. The twins could play major college football and still receive a quality education. (At the time, neither was thinking about a career in the NFL.) In addition, Tiki loved the school's architecture, its aura of history, and its diversity.

The Barbers had until early 1993 to choose a school, but they made their decision in November 1992. Danny Wilmer was the lucky recruiter who signed the twins. After landing their commitments, Wilmer shared the good news with Virginia head coach George Welsh during a staff meeting.

"Both of them?" Welsh asked, as reported in *The Virginian-Pilot.*

Wilmer nodded.

"Geez, Danny," Welsh said with a smile. "Way to go!"

At the time, Welsh knew he had landed two talented twins, but he had no idea that they would become the cornerstone of the Virginia football program. Back in Roanoke, in the late summer of 1993, Geraldine watched in sadness as her sons packed their suitcases. She couldn't have been more proud. But, as reported on ESPN.com, it was "emotional for me when [Tiki] and Ronde left for college," she said. "I was left with an empty house. My two sons were gone."

Fortunately, Gerry had raised her sons well. Though the twins would live 120 miles (193 kilometers) away in Charlottesville, the Barbers would remain a tight-knit family—through college and beyond.

The Barbers
of C'Ville

Shoot for the moon. That was Tiki Barber's philosophy when he first stepped on the campus of the University of Virginia. "I wanted to be an aerospace engineer at first," he told *U.S. News & World Report,* "so I could be an astronaut."

Soon, Barber's otherworldly dream dissipated. Although he would rocket down the football field and fly through the air as a record-setting long jumper, his career ambition became more modest. Barber became enamored with computers and the challenge of writing code. He transferred out of the engineering school and into the McIntire School of Commerce. He thought seriously about a future in information technology; i.e., computers.

For his first two years on campus, Barber blended in with the crowd. Though Virginia competed in the highly respected Atlantic Coast Conference, it was not a "football school." It was a prestigious university that strongly emphasized academics over athletics. In fact, instead of wearing the Cavaliers' team colors to football games, the students dressed as if it was a formal school event. "[T]he student body wore khakis, ties, button-up shirts with tennis shoes, and baseball caps at football games," Barber recalled in *U.S. News & World Report.* "I thought they looked ridiculous, but apparently it was some kind of tradition."

Barber didn't play much football as a freshman, carrying the ball just 16 times for 45 yards. However, he loved the excitement of college life—from the challenge of schoolwork to meeting new people. "I loved the diversity," he told the *U.S. News* reporter. "It was such a melting pot of people, religions, etc." Tiki and Ronde shared a suite and hung in the same circles. On weekends, the brothers walked down Rugby Road to party at the fraternity houses. The once-shy Tiki certainly broke out of his shell, although eventually the brothers tired of the frat-party scene.

As a sophomore in the fall of 1994, Tiki played a bit more at tailback and excelled as a **kick returner**. In fact, he earned All-ACC honorable mention honors. Yet in his memoir, Barber barely mentions his sophomore season, writing instead about a young woman whom he first spotted in his computer science class.

Tiki eyed Virginia "Ginny" Joy Cha throughout the winter semester in 1995. But only through an incredible stroke of luck did he get to talk to her. His friend James happened to ask out Ginny's roommate, who felt uncomfortable going out alone with James. Thus, Tiki and Ginny came along for support. As the foursome dined at the Outback Steakhouse, Tiki connected immediately with Ginny, whom he found to be smart, witty, and full of energy. Only one problem: She had a boyfriend.

By the following fall, however, Ginny and Tiki began to date. Tiki was fascinated by her background. Her father,

Won Cha, had grown up in communist North Korea before secretly swimming to freedom in South Korea. He eventually landed work as an engineer with the U.S. government in South Vietnam during the war in that country. He married a Vietnamese woman named Nga and escaped South Vietnam in 1975, just days before communist North Vietnam took over the country. The couple settled in Washington, D.C, and named their second daughter after the state of Virginia. Over the years, Ginny's father became a devoted fan of professional football. Yet he never dreamed that, one day, he would become the father-in-law of an NFL star.

AGONY AND ECSTASY

Ronde enjoyed his breakout season as a sophomore. He intercepted eight passes—second most in the nation—and was named a third-team All-American. Tiki emerged as a star early in his *junior* season. Real early. August 26, to be exact.

Though extremely fast, Tiki had not earned many carries as a sophomore because he weighed only 175 pounds. However, he added 15 pounds of muscle for the new season. After Virginia's starting tailback pulled a **hamstring**, Barber got the call to start the opening game of the 1995 campaign.

This was no ordinary Virginia football game. The Cavaliers traveled to the "Big House" to play mighty Michigan in front of more than 100,000 maize-and-blue diehards. Dubbed the Pigskin Classic, the nationally televised game was the first matchup of the college football season.

On the journey to Ann Arbor, Barber experienced a screaming headache that would not go away. The team doctor responded with antibiotics and an IV. Although he barely slept that night, Barber felt rejuvenated the next day and was ready to go.

Stunningly, Virginia took a 17-0 lead against the Wolverines. Ronde contributed with an **interception**, and Tiki made the play of the game. On third down at the Cavaliers' 19-yard line,

University of Michigan defender Tyrone Noble dives in an attempt to tackle Tiki Barber during the Virginia-Michigan game on August 26, 1995, in Ann Arbor. In the game, Barber rushed for an 81-yard touchdown but also separated his shoulder when he was hit by a linebacker on the same play.

Tiki absorbed a brutal hit from Jarrett Irons, one of the most ferocious **linebackers** in Michigan history. The blow separated Barber's shoulder, but he kept on running. In fact, he raced 81 yards for a touchdown.

Tiki could not play anymore, and on the sidelines he watched Michigan stage a dramatic comeback. The Wolverines scored 18 fourth-quarter points, including a touchdown on the last play of the game to tie and an **extra point** to win it. For Barber, it was a weekend of pain and agony—with euphoric glory in between.

TIKI VS. GOLIATH

Tiki, who quickly recovered from his separated shoulder, proved to be the real deal at running back. With his exceptional vision and patience, he was able to hit the right holes. And with his explosive quickness, he got there in a hurry. Barber also had the jets to blast downfield, and his outstanding receiving skills added a further dimension to his game.

Barber's coach, George Welsh, compared his moves to those of Emmitt Smith, who was on his way to becoming the NFL's all-time leading rusher. "[Tiki] went from being a good outside runner to being a big-league tailback," Welsh told *The Virginian-Pilot*. "He is pretty clever, and I am not sure I have ever coached a running back quite like him before."

The Cavaliers enjoyed one of their greatest seasons ever in 1995, and Tiki and Ronde led the way. Together, they were called "The Barbers of C'Ville"—a play on the opera *The Barber of Seville*. Tiki grabbed the lion's share of the headlines in Charlottesville. In seven straight games, he rushed for more than 100 yards. Against Duke, he burned the Blue Demons for 185 yards rushing. Virginia lost only three times, and two of those were on the last plays of the game—to powerhouses Michigan and Texas.

On November 2, Virginia hosted Florida State in a nationally televised Thursday night matchup. The Cavaliers were unranked, but their heroic play had won the support of the student body. Although it rained all day, the student sections at Scott Stadium filled up three hours before kickoff.

Virginia seemingly had no chance of beating the Seminoles. From 1987 through 1999, coach Bobby Bowden's team was among the best in the land, never finishing lower than fourth in the season-ending Associated Press poll. Entering the Virginia game, the Seminoles were 7–0 and ranked No. 2. UVA had never beaten Florida State, and Florida State had not lost to an ACC school since joining the conference four years earlier. So far in 1995, the Seminoles had destroyed Duke 70-26, North Carolina State 77-17, and Wake Forest 72-13.

Barber **fumbled** on Virginia's first possession, and sure enough Florida State capitalized with a touchdown. If the Cavaliers were somehow to compete against this football Goliath, Welsh believed, he would have to empty his bag of tricks. On the next series, he surprised the Seminoles with an **option** play—in which the quarterback runs toward the sideline and has the option of running with the ball himself or pitching it to his tailback. Quarterback Mike Groh pitched it to Barber, who ran 64 yards for a touchdown. The fans went berserk.

The Cavs' confidence soared, and Welsh continued to outwit the Seminoles with unexpected plays. They tried the option again as well as **draw plays**, **screen plays**, and **rollout passes**. The star-studded Florida State defense could not find a way to stop Barber. He rushed for 193 yards, and he caught a pass for a touchdown. His rushing, reception, and kick-return gains added up to 301 yards.

With 80 seconds left in the game, Virginia led 33-28 and the Seminoles had the ball deep in their own territory. But they drove all the way down the field, reaching the 6-yard line with four seconds left. It came down to one last play. Fans, having already stormed the field before being shooed back, now prayed for one last miracle. On the sideline, Barber and his teammates held hands.

In a bizarre trick play, the Florida State **center** snapped the ball not to the quarterback but to Warrick Dunn. The All-American running back angled right and seemingly into the **end zone**—until **safety** Adrian Burnim came out of the blue and stopped him cold at the 1-foot line. The game was over. Fans stormed the field again. Virginia had pulled off one of the most stunning upsets of the decade. Not surprisingly, Barber calls it the greatest moment of his college career.

University of Virginia fans tear down a goalpost on November 2, 1995, after the Cavaliers upset the No. 2-ranked Florida State Seminoles 33-28. Tiki Barber rushed for 193 yards in the game; with receptions and kickoff returns, he had 301 total yards.

MAINTAINING PERSPECTIVE

In the delirious aftermath of the game, Barber spotted a former buddy of his on the field. Lou had been a close, platonic female friend of his during their freshman years. "I love you," she yelled to him during the chaos, as Barber recounted in his memoir. "You're awesome." Barber half-noticed Lou, but instead of seeking her out, he went to celebrate with his team-mates. Two weeks later, she died in a fire.

Lou's death profoundly affected Tiki. He berated himself for how he had responded to her after the game and wondered if he had let his ego get the best of him. He cried uncontrollable tears, and he resolved never to put football or fame above human decency.

When the season ended, Barber had to do a whole lot of ego taming. His accomplishments and awards were overwhelming. He had rushed for 14 touchdowns and 1,397 yards, a school record, while averaging 5.3 yards per carry. He was named first-team All-ACC, and he earned honorable-mention All-American kudos from *Football News*. He was honored as Virginia's Most Outstanding Player, and he was named a finalist for the Doak Walker Award, given to the nation's premier running back.

Not long after Lou's death, Tiki and Ronde heard the worst news of their lives: Their mother had been diagnosed with breast cancer. Tiki, of course, was devastated. "I went through self-pity, denial, and depression," he wrote in his memoir. "Without my mother, I would be a puzzle with a large piece missing. The equation was always Mom + Ronde + me. Three legs of a stool. Take away one, and the whole thing collapses."

Gerry also got angry and depressed, as most cancer patients do. But then, as she recounted in an article on Mosaec.com, she realized that "I've got a life to live. Rather than sitting around trying to figure out when [life] is going to end, I'm going to enjoy it while I can."

Once again, Mom amazed her children with her courage and determination. Chemotherapy was an agonizing process, yet she planned her sessions around her sons' football schedule so that she would not miss any games. Her oncologist had never seen anyone do anything like that.

Just one day after undergoing a mastectomy (in the fall of Tiki's senior season), Gerry left the hospital because she could not take everyone crying around her. Four days later, she climbed the stairs of Scott Stadium to watch her sons play football. Tiki looked up at the most courageous person he had ever known, and cried. (Gerry has been cancer-free since her treatment.)

DEATH OF A DREAM

Tiki has rarely talked about it, but early in his college career he dreamed of competing in the Summer Olympics. This wasn't one of those far-off fantasies, like becoming an astronaut, but a legitimate ambition. As mentioned, he had finished second in the long jump in the national high school finals in 1992.

Barber continued to tear up the track as a college freshman. In his very first attempt, he tied the school record in the long jump, soaring 24 feet, 6 inches (7.46 meters). He lettered in track for three years, once finishing second in the long jump at the IC4A Indoor Championships. This event pitted the best athletes from numerous Eastern universities.

Barber also had astonishing speed. He ran the 40-yard dash in 4.28 seconds, setting a record for Virginia football players that has yet to be broken. As a sophomore, Tiki and Ronde made up half of the 4x100-meter relay team that finished fifth at the 1995 ACC Outdoor Championships.

That spring, Tiki faced a crossroads. Ken Mack, Virginia's running backs coach, told Barber that he needed to muscle up. If not, he said, he would not likely play much at running back. Mack wanted him to beef up by 25 pounds, from 175 to 200. Barber knew that all of those extra pounds would destroy his long-jump career—and kill his Olympic dream.

Barber had to choose between track and football. He chose the latter, adding 15 pounds in the weight room by the time

Tiki Barber cuts back to avoid a tackle during a game on November 21, 1995, against the Wake Forest Demon Deacons. During the 1995 season, Barber rushed for a school-record 1,397 yards. The following season, his senior year, he nearly matched that total, with 1,360 yards. His college career over, Barber next anticipated where he would go in the NFL Draft.

the 1995 Pigskin Classic kicked off. Barber would never regret his decision, especially after he busted through the Michigan defense for his 81-yard run. After his junior year, he quit track for good.

CLOSING THE BOOK AT UVA

With his mind on his mother, Tiki struggled to focus on football during his senior season. Nevertheless, he continued to put up impressive numbers. His 1,360 yards rushing nearly matched his record-setting total of a year earlier, and he upped his rushing average one tick to 5.4 yards per carry. Though Virginia could not match its 1995 success, Tiki repeated as a first-team All-ACC selection. Meanwhile, Ronde made first-team all-conference for the third straight season.

After their final football season, the twins concentrated on their studies. Ronde graduated with a degree in commerce, while Tiki earned his degree in management information systems. Even Geraldine hit the books. She enrolled at Averett

THE NFL DRAFT

The toughest part about being a football fan is waiting from February to September to see NFL action. Fortunately, there's the NFL Draft—the most anticipated draft of all the major sports. On the last weekend of April, NFL executives gather in New York City, team leaders huddle in their "war rooms," and fans anxiously watch events unfold on ESPN.

To achieve competitive balance within the league, the NFL (like the other major sports leagues) awards the No. 1 pick to the team with the worst record. The second-worst team picks second, and so on. In the first round, each team gets 10 minutes to announce its selection. Teams get seven minutes to decide on their second-round picks and five minutes for rounds three through seven (the last round). The whole process takes two exhausting days.

In 1997, NFL Commissioner Paul Tagliabue announced that Orlando Pace—a massive offensive tackle from Ohio State—was the first overall pick, taken by the St. Louis Rams. The Giants, who picked seventh in the first round, actually considered selecting Tiki Barber with that pick. Giants head coach Jim

College in Danville, Virginia, where she pursued a master's degree in business.

But before graduation, the Barbers braced for an event that would determine the rest of their careers: NFL **Draft** Day. The twins knew that they would be drafted. Tiki, scouts said, would probably go late in the first round or early in the second. Ronde probably would be selected a round or so after his brother. Tiki hoped that the Washington Redskins,

Fassel, in his debut season, wanted to make a splash by landing a flashy play-maker.

Selecting Barber, a little scatback, that high would have shocked the draft pundits. Giants running backs coach Jim Skipper told Fassel to hold off—that Barber would still be available in the second round. Instead, the Giants spent their first-round pick on Florida receiver Ike Hilliard, who has had a fine but injury-plagued career.

Had Barber gone seventh overall, his agent would have demanded—and received—much more money for his client. Hilliard signed a six-year, $12 million contract after being drafted, while Barber's contract included a $705,000 signing bonus and just a $320,000 salary for the first year.

Expectations for Barber would have been much higher, however, and he would have been labeled a "bust" during his first few years. In retrospect, Barber said, he is glad the draft worked out as it did. He has always liked being the underdog, overcoming obstacles to emerge on top. And besides, he eventually made his millions.

his favorite team growing up, would select him, but they weren't interested. Instead, the Green Bay Packers and the San Francisco 49ers had their eye on him.

In his heart, Tiki wished that Charlottesville, Virginia, had an NFL team. While he was headed to some undoubtedly far-off city, his girlfriend, Ginny, still had a year of school ahead of her. Barber knew that he wanted to keep her in his life, even if they had to maintain a long-distance relationship for a year.

Ginny did not want to break up with Tiki, but she was also practical about her future. She yearned to pursue a career in the fashion industry, which likely meant she would have to go to New York City. On the night before the draft, as they discussed their future during dinner at the Golden Corral, Ginny told Tiki that she could not picture herself in Green Bay—or even San Francisco. Tiki feared that they would drift apart for good.

The next day, NFL personnel would determine where Tiki and Ronde would spend the next few years of their lives. Maybe Tiki would wind up in Arizona or Seattle, a million miles from his twin brother and the woman he loved. Who knew? The Barber brothers could not deal with all the Draft Day anxiety, so they went golfing.

On the 17th green, Tiki sank his first birdie putt of the day. As he shook his fist in triumph, his cell phone rang. On the other end was a public relations guy named Pat Hanlon, who told Tiki that he was about to put coach Jim Fassel on the phone. Fassel told Barber that he admired his talents and that he was about to draft him with the next pick in the second round. That sounded good to Barber, but who was Jim Fassel and which team did he represent? Eventually he figured it out. Fassel was the head coach of the New York Giants.

Tiki's first thought, literally, was that he and Ginny could be in New York together, pursuing their dreams. He could not wait to tell her, and when she found out, she was equally thrilled.

Later in the day, the Barbers celebrated more great news: Ronde was drafted in the third round by the Tampa Bay Buccaneers.

That evening, Tiki and Ronde sat down with Gerry at dinner. All their lives, they had watched their mother work day and night and weekends to provide for them. For so many years, they wished they could ease her burden. Tiki leaned toward his mother. "Mom," he said, according to an article on Mosaec.com, "I want you to quit your job tomorrow. Ronde and I will take care of you."

For Tiki Barber—and Ronde and Gerry and Ginny, too—it could not have been a sweeter day.

Early Struggles in New York

Tiki Barber had never liked New York. For his tastes, it was far too congested, noisy, dirty, smelly. When he first experienced Manhattan—traveling with Ginny in January 1997 to visit her sister—a blizzard sacked the city. The couple slept on Sis's floor in a cramped studio apartment, for which she undoubtedly paid a fortune.

The New York Giants did not actually play in New York. They toiled in Giants Stadium in East Rutherford, New Jersey. Barber, too, avoided the big city, renting an apartment along the Hudson River in Jersey City, New Jersey. Barber felt that he had the best of both worlds: He enjoyed a sensational view of Manhattan across the water, but he did not have to live there.

As an NFL **rookie**, Barber never felt more alone. For the first time in his life, he lived outside of his home state and—

more significant—away from his twin brother. Ginny, the love of his life, was back on campus in Charlottesville beginning her senior year. The Giants trained in Albany, New York, where Barber was not just a rookie but also one of the smallest men on the team. As a high second-round pick, Barber was expected to perform immediately. But Rodney Hampton, one of the greatest running backs in Giants history, ranked ahead of him on the depth chart. So, too, did Tyrone Wheatley, a powerful third-year back who had contended for the **Heisman Trophy** at Michigan.

Nevertheless, new coach Jim Fassel liked what Barber brought to the table. A "jitterbug" back, Barber darted through holes in a flash and juked linebackers out of their shoes. After Hampton went down with an injury, Barber entered the starting lineup on Opening Day.

Barber surprised even himself in his very first game. Against the Philadelphia Eagles, he took 20 handoffs and ran for 88 yards—twice ripping off big runs. Barber tacked on 32 receiving yards and even scored a touchdown.

Reality, however, kicked in the following week. Although he scored again, Barber mustered just 17 yards on 11 carries versus Jacksonville. Against St. Louis in Week 4, he carried the ball nine times for an embarrassing four yards. The next week, the New Orleans Saints added injury to insult. Barber tore the posterior cruciate **ligament** in his right knee.

It was the lowest point in Barber's career. He had struggled enough on healthy knees; how could he possibly perform on a gimpy one? Strong knees were especially important to Barber, who relied on sharp cuts to elude tacklers. Unsure if he would ever make it in the NFL, Barber began to think about other careers—perhaps in business or broadcasting.

Barber returned in Week 11 but only in a limited role. In his first four games upon his return, he totaled just 68 yards rushing. Only a big outing in Week 15—114 yards rushing against the Eagles—helped him restore some faith. The Giants made the playoffs with a 10–5–1 record, but they lost a heart-breaker in the **wild-card** game to Minnesota, 23-22.

Considering the injury and other lowlights, Barber put up respectable numbers for a rookie. His 511 rushing yards ranked third among first-year players in the **National Football Conference** (NFC), and his 810 yards from scrimmage (rushing

HISTORY OF THE NEW YORK GIANTS

Back in 1925, businessman Tim Mara pulled out $500 and bought a professional football team. At that time, teams played in such blue-collar towns as Dayton, Ohio, and Rochester, New York. Mara thought it would be a smart investment to start an NFL franchise in New York City—and, boy, was he right. Decades later, fans would spend $500 just for a single Giants Super Bowl ticket.

They called Mara's ball club the New York Football Giants, to distinguish them from the New York Giants, who dominated baseball's National League in the 1920s. The footballers went 11–1–1 and romped to the NFL title in 1927. However, the 1929 stock-market crash affected Mara so severely that he handed the Giants over to his sons, Jack (age 22) and Wellington (just 14) to insulate the team from creditors. Wellington became a co-owner of the team in 1959, after his father's death, and remained in that position until his own death in 2005.

For years, the two Giants teams shared the Polo Grounds in New York City. The footballers took the NFL title in 1934 thanks to a win over Chicago in the famous "Sneakers Game." With the temperature a frigid 9°F (-13°C) and the turf frozen solid, the Giants put on basketball shoes at halftime for better and receiving) ranked second among rookies. His next season, however, was a whole different story.

SOPHOMORE SLUMP

In the early months of 1998, Barber looked forward to the spring thaw. Ginny was about to graduate from Virginia, and that meant she could move to New York. She looked forward

traction. New York overcame a 10-3 deficit and sprinted to a 30-13 victory.

The Giants repeated as NFL champs in 1938 and again in 1956, when halfback extraordinaire Frank Gifford won the NFL MVP Award. From 1961 to 1963, quarterback Y.A. Tittle fired 86 touchdown passes and took the Giants to three NFL championship games, but they lost them all. From there, the franchise slugged through two decades of misery.

The Giants not only struggled in the 1970s, but they also bounced from one home to another. The team moved from Yankee Stadium to the Yale Bowl in Connecticut to Shea Stadium in New York City to the Meadowlands in East Rutherford, New Jersey. Only in the mid-1980s, under the leadership of browbeating coach Bill Parcells and bone-crushing linebacker Lawrence Taylor, did the Giants emerge as a contender. New York whipped Denver 39-20 in the Super Bowl in January 1987 and nipped Buffalo 20-19 on Super Bowl Sunday in 1991. The Giants have been up and down ever since, hitting peaks in 2000 with a Super Bowl appearance and, in 2007, with their Super Bowl victory over the previously undefeated New England Patriots.

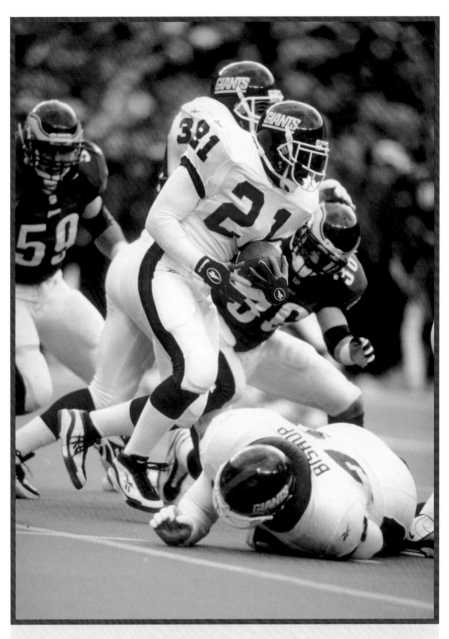

During his rookie season, Tiki Barber had his two best games against the Philadelphia Eagles—rushing for 88 yards in the season opener and for 114 yards in a game on December 7. Here, Barber gains some of those rushing yards in the December contest. In between the two games, Barber was out for several weeks after he tore a ligament in his knee.

to it, especially after Tiki suggested that they move to the city itself—not the outskirts. When Ginny landed an entry-level job in the fashion industry, both seemed to be fulfilling their dreams—or so they thought.

Ginny wound up working day and night, crimping their relationship. Tiki, in contrast, was not working enough. While Ronde enjoyed a breakthrough season in 1998, cracking the starting the lineup, Tiki barely played. Running back Rodney Hampton had retired, but Barber simply was not good enough to fill his shoes.

After totaling 25 carries his first two games, for just 69 yards, Barber averaged just two rushes per outing over the rest of the season. Coach Fassel used him only on short-yardage and third-down situations, where he valued Barber's playmaking skills. Barber did catch 42 passes for 348 yards, and he returned 14 **kickoffs**. However, his 166 yards rushing disappointed everyone—especially himself. The team's mediocre 8–8 record did not help matters.

Barber lost his enthusiasm for the game, and he moped at practice and on the sidelines. Finally, prior to the next season, Fassel sat down and talked with his young running back. "Tiki, I like you," said Fassel, as recounted by Barber in his memoir. "You're like my own kid." Tiki braced for the inevitable criticism. "I want you to focus on a different role," Fassel said, "because you're not doing good at being the every-down back."

Fassel clearly defined Barber's new role. He wanted him to pour his energies into being a third-down running back and the team's main punt-return guy. From that point on, Barber no longer moped. Instead, he worked hard to be the best third-down back and punt returner in the NFL.

A NEW ATTITUDE

Barber's life changed dramatically in 1999. It all began with the phone call from Greg Comella, which triggered his grueling but life-altering hill-climbing routine. As the year progressed, Barber took on other challenges as well.

First, he made his acting debut in an off-Broadway play. The low-budget *Seeing Double* began in February and ran for 16 performances at the New Amsterdam Café. In this comedy, a pair of female twins lived with one of their boyfriends. Barber played the part of the boyfriend's lawyer. Why was an NFL running back performing in a play at a neighborhood café? "I wasn't a big-time football player," Barber said in *The New Yorker*. "I was just trying to make it. I had no idea what my career would be like."

Working with a young agent named Mark Lepselter, Barber began to break into broadcasting. He volunteered his time to the sports radio station WFAN, and he did local sports news for another station at 5:00 A.M.

On May 15, 1999, Barber took another leap of faith. In the chapel at the University of Virginia, he and Ginny exchanged vows. It had poured the day before, but the sun shone brightly on their wedding day. The ceremony was attended by 150 people, with Ronde—of course—serving as best man.

Before the 1999 season, Coach Fassel told reporters that Barber "needs to improve if we're going to get better." Barber was determined and prepared to do just that. As expected, he didn't get many carries—just 62 all season while playing primarily as a third-down back. But his strength-training on the hill of Ramapo paid off. Barber rushed for 4.2 yards per carry, a full yard better than his previous season.

More impressive, Barber caught 66 passes, which set a Giants record for a back. Using his open-field running skills, he turned those receptions into 609 yards. Barber, who returned a few kickoffs for the Giants, also became a potent weapon as a punt returner.

Tiki had never returned **punts** in the NFL before, and he did not exactly relish the experience. In his memoir, he recalled waiting forever for the punted ball to float down into his arms

During a 1999 game against the Dallas Cowboys, Tiki Barber celebrates his 85-yard punt return for a touchdown with teammates Bashir Levingston *(center)* and David Patten *(left)*. Barber also had a key reception that led to the Giants' game-winning field goal in the October 18 contest. The Giants beat the Cowboys 13-10.

while 10 muscle-bound brutes torpedoed downfield—with him as the target. His "strategy" was to make a move or two and then hope for the best.

On October 18 against Dallas, on *Monday Night Football,* Barber returned a punt all the way for a touchdown. His good buddy, Greg Comella, executed the block that set Barber free. He ran 85 yards for the Giants' only touchdown of the day. He also turned a pass reception into a 56-yard gain, which set up New York's game-winning **field goal**.

In Week 14, Barber caught eight passes in New York's 19-17 upset over Buffalo. The victory put the Giants' record at 7–6, but they dropped the last three games to fall out of the playoff picture.

After fretting about Y2K and then celebrating the arrival of the year 2000, New Yorkers gave little heed to the Giants' last game of the 1999 season, played on January 2, 2000. Fans expected more mediocrity from the Giants the following season. A trip to the Super Bowl was the last thing on their minds.

Rushing to the
Super Bowl

To the casual fan, it appeared that Tiki Barber's 1999 rushing total of 258 yards might dwindle in the new season. After all, the Giants selected Wisconsin running back Ron Dayne with the eleventh pick in the first round of the 2000 NFL Draft. Like Barber, Dayne stood a modest 5-foot-10—but he weighed 253 pounds. More important, the "Great Dayne" had rushed for a staggering 6,397 yards in college, breaking the NCAA Division 1-A career rushing record.

Many NFL coaches would have designed their offense around the reliable Dayne. But the Giants, who had run a conservative offense the previous year with poor results, wanted to mix things up. Before the 2000 season, the Giants promoted quarterbacks coach Sean Payton to offensive coordinator.

Called a coaching genius by Barber, Payton proceeded to energize the New York offense.

A young, innovative coach, Payton would study film late into the evening and then sleep overnight at the stadium. Yet he would awake in the morning full of energy—and ideas. Barber loved him, especially because he made Tiki an integral part of the offense. No longer would he just be used on third-down and passing situations. Instead, he and Dayne would share the ball-lugging duties. The rookie would bull up the middle, while Barber would zip around the end or carry the ball on a **misdirection play**. Misdirection turned out to be a potent weapon for the Giants. With everyone moving toward one side, Barber would cut back and go the other way.

Payton called his two running backs "Thunder and Lightning." Barber liked being the lightning part of the duo because, while thunder is scary, lightning is deadly!

Fans, however, were skeptical, especially after New York lost all four of its preseason games. The new offense, however, worked beautifully in the season opener—especially for Barber. After scoring on a 10-yard run in the first quarter, he burst through the middle for a 78-yard romp in the second. It was the fourth-longest run in Giants history. Barber rushed for a career-high 144 yards on 13 carries to help New York knock off Arizona 21-16. "I have been talking all preseason about how excited I am about this offense," Barber said after game. "Coach Payton is going to give me the ball in situations where I can make the big plays happen."

Though Payton gave him the opportunities, Barber himself made things happen. The hill-climbing had made him stronger, and three years of studying film and technique had given him a mental edge. Barber ran to daylight the next week, too, amassing 96 yards on just 11 carries as New York routed Philadelphia 33-18. "They make it hard to get a bead on what they're going to do," Eagles defensive end Hugh Douglas said in the *Sporting*

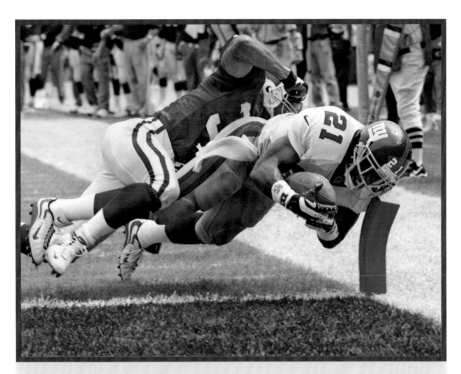

Arizona Cardinals cornerback Aeneas Williams fails to stop Tiki Barber from diving over the goal line to score a 10-yard touchdown in the first quarter of a game on September 3, 2000, at Giants Stadium. In the second quarter, Barber had a 78-yard run, the fourth-longest in Giants history.

News. "Everything looks like the other thing. They make the pass look like the run and vice versa."

The next week against Chicago, Barber rushed for 86 yards on 17 carries and totaled 58 receiving yards. When he scored on a three-yard misdirection handoff, it gave him four touchdowns in three games. The Giants won again, 14-7. Through three games, Barber had averaged 109 yards per game and an eye-popping 8.0 yards per carry. A star was born.

CRACKING 1,000

Although Barber could not maintain that pace for the rest of the season, he continued to produce solid numbers. Eleven times he exceeded 50 yards rushing, and nine times he eclipsed 40 yards receiving. For the first time since Barber's rookie season, the Giants played like contenders. Kerry Collins, with 22 touchdown passes and just 13 interceptions, provided a steady hand at quarterback. Meanwhile, the defense, spearheaded by linebacker Jessie Armstead, proved impenetrable. New York jumped out to a 7–2 start before dropping a pair of games at home.

After losing to Detroit to fall to 7–4, head coach Jim Fassel guaranteed that his team would make the playoffs. The coach proved prophetic, as New York rolled to victory in its next five games. The Giants proved to be great road soldiers, going 7–1 in enemy stadiums. Barber evolved into a warrior of his own. After breaking a bone in his left forearm during the Dallas game (the season's second-to-last game), the team doctor told him he would be out six weeks. Barber said no way; he wasn't going to miss the playoffs. So his damaged arm was wrapped in a soft cast, and he played the next week in the season finale.

Displaying true grit, he rushed for 78 yards on a season-high 24 carries in a 28-25 win over Jacksonville. He finished the season with 1,006 yards rushing, nearly quadrupling his total from the previous year. Only five other backs in Giants history had ever eclipsed 1,000 yards rushing: Ron Johnson, Joe Morris, Ottis Anderson, Rodney Hampton, and Gary Brown. Moreover, with his 719 receiving yards, as well as his gains on punt returns, Barber finished with a whopping 2,085 **all-purpose yards**, breaking the team record by a full 278 yards.

Barber had become the marquee attraction on a high-profile playoff team. Kids in New York, New Jersey, and all over the country began to idolize the exciting halfback with the funny name: Tiki Barber!

STORMING THROUGH THE PLAYOFFS

The Giants not only made the playoffs, but their 12–4 record was also the best in the National Football Conference. That

Tiki Barber sweeps in for the first touchdown of the game in the 2000 season finale between the Giants and the Jacksonville Jaguars. Barber finished the regular season with 2,085 all-purpose yards—breaking a team record.

earned them a bye during the first week of the postseason and gave them home-field advantage throughout the playoffs. To top it off, they got to play Philadelphia in their first postseason game—a team they had beaten eight consecutive times.

Yet it proved to be a struggle. The Eagles contained the New York offense, keeping it out of the end zone for four quarters. Barber could not get untracked, rushing for just 35 yards on 15 carries. Nevertheless, the Giants' Ron Dixon scored on a kickoff return, and Jason Sehorn returned an interception for a touchdown. The Giants prevailed 20-10, earning a spot in the NFC Championship Game.

Some cynics still did not believe in the Giants, saying they had lucked into the conference title game. But the Giants believed in themselves, and they entered the contest against Minnesota in high spirits. Before the game, Barber acquired a replica jersey of the Vikings' star **wide receiver**, Randy Moss, and printed the Super Bowl XXXV logo onto it. He also attached a quotation to the jersey, one from Civil War General Ulysses S. Grant. It read: "The art of war is simple enough. Find out where your enemy is. Get to him as soon as you can. Strike at him as hard as you can, and keep moving on."

It wasn't the first motivational message, or prop, that Barber had left in the Giants' locker room, but it may have been the most audacious. As it turned out, it seemed to curse the All-Pro receiver. Moss caught just two passes in the game for a measly 18 yards.

With Giants fans clad in team colors and waving towels, New York slammed the favored Vikings like a blue tornado. Within the first 2:13 of the first quarter, quarterback Kerry Collins fired touchdown strikes to receiver Ike Hilliard and fullback Greg Comella—Barber's good friend. On this day, the Giants did not need to rely on "Thunder and Lightning." Instead, Collins exploited Minnesota's injury-depleted secondary. In the first half alone, he threw for 338 yards and four touchdowns. Shockingly, the Giants ran off the field at halftime with a 34-0 lead.

Collins threw another touchdown pass early in the third quarter, and New York prevailed 41-0. Barber's fine performance, 69 yards on 12 carries, was barely discussed, but he

TIKI'S FAVORITES

Culled from various interviews Tiki Barber has given, here are a few of his favorite things:

Person He Most Admires: His mother, Geraldine Barber-Hale

Favorite Player Growing Up: Running back Walter Payton

Favorite Team as a Kid: Washington Redskins

Favorite Hobbies: Reading, golfing, Web surfing

Favorite Food: Kobe steak

Favorite Home-Cooked Meal: Kim and bap (seaweed and rice)

Favorite College Achievements: Beating Florida State and creating his own Web site

Favorite Family Outing: New York's Central Park Zoo (as of 2004)

Favorite Movie: *The Goonies*

Favorite Musician: Lenny Kravitz

Favorite Car: The Maybach

Best Advice He Ever Received: Never stop believing in yourself

Favorite Motto: Live as if you'll die tomorrow, and learn as if you'll live forever

Two Dreams He Achieved: Starring as a running back in the NFL and working on the *Today* show

Craziest Ambition: Competing in a triathlon

Favorite Quotation: "A man who has never gone to school may steal from a freight car; but if he has a university education, he may steal the whole railroad."—said by Theodore Roosevelt could not care less. To this day, he considers the game the most exciting of his NFL career.

"It was the perfect game," Barber said in *Men's Fitness* magazine. "It was at home, the biggest game you can play at Giants Stadium. Everything we did was so perfect it was like a high school game for us. To see 80,000 people have that energy and excitement and throw it all down onto you . . . it was euphoric. I'd call it euphoria."

Afterward, the Giants celebrated to the song "Glory Days," by New Jersey native Bruce Springsteen. Team owner Wellington Mara, age 84, revved up the party with his postgame speech. "This team was referred to as the worst team ever to win the home-field advantage in the National Football League," Mara declared. "And today, on our field of painted mud, we proved that we're the worst team ever to win the National Football Conference championship. In two weeks, we're going to try to become the worst team ever to win the Super Bowl."

SUPER FRUSTRATION

One year earlier, Barber had attended the Super Bowl, sitting in Ginny's company box. "[I]t was awesome," Tiki recalled in *People* magazine. "I told Ginny, 'I've got to play in this game!' But I didn't think it would happen so soon!"

Super Bowl XXXV—the Giants versus the Baltimore Ravens—was staged in Tampa, Florida, home of Ronde Barber's Tampa Bay Buccaneers. Reporters had a storyline: Tiki aims for glory in his twin brother's backyard. While the press peppered the pair with questions, Ronde gave the most prophetic response. "If he loses this year," he said in *People*, "then I'll have to go win it next year."

Tiki knew he would have to fight for his yardage against Baltimore. The Ravens not only had the best defense in the NFL, but they were also the only team ever to yield fewer than 1,000 yards rushing over a 16-game schedule. After the

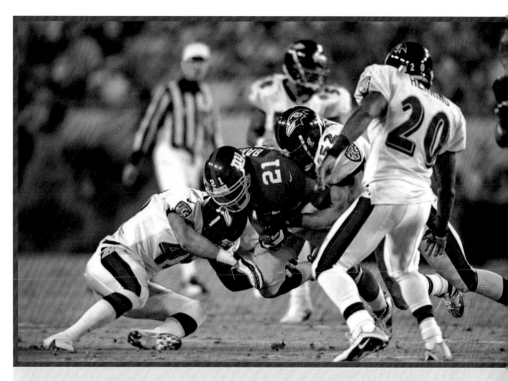

Baltimore Ravens linebacker Ray Lewis *(center)* and safety Corey Harris *(left)* tackle Tiki Barber during Super Bowl XXXV, played on January 28, 2001, in Tampa, Florida. Although Barber rushed for 49 yards and caught six passes for 26 yards, the Giants fell to the Ravens 34-7.

elaborate pregame festivities—with the Backstreet Boys singing the national anthem—Super Bowl XXXV got underway.

Unfortunately for Giants fans, the game turned out to be one long frustration. With New York down 7-0 in the second quarter, linebacker Jessie Armstead seemingly returned an interception 43 yards for a touchdown—but it was called back because of a **holding penalty**. Barber ripped off a 27-yard run in the second quarter, but on the next play Collins threw an interception. After New York's Ron Dixon returned a kickoff 97 yards for a touchdown, Baltimore's Jermaine Lewis scored on the very next kickoff to put the Ravens up 23-7. That sealed the deal, as Baltimore won 34-7.

Even though the Giants offense did not score, Barber performed well. He rushed for 49 yards on 11 carries and caught six passes for 26 yards. As for his brother's pregame comments, Ronde and the Buccaneers did win the Super Bowl—not the following season but a year after that. In Super Bowl XXXVII, Tampa Bay routed Oakland 48-21, with Tiki cheering from the stands.

Busting Loose

After the 2000 season, Tiki Barber entered contract negotiations with the Giants. He wanted to remain with the team for a long time, and the feeling was, of course, mutual. The two sides agreed to a deal that would pay Barber $25 million over six years. Tiki and future generations of Barbers were set for life. After signing the contract, he called himself "the happiest man in New York right now."

Unfortunately, the euphoria of the Super Bowl and the contract wore off early in the 2001 season. The Giants lost the season opener to Denver, with Barber rushing for just 28 yards. Then, the next day, on September 11, tragedy struck. Terrorists in hijacked jets struck the Twin Towers of the World Trade Center in Manhattan, just a few miles from Barber's home. The two towers collapsed. Another hijacked jet hit the Pentagon near Washington, D.C., and a fourth plane taken over by terrorists crashed in a field in Pennsylvania.

The tragedy profoundly affected all Americans, including the Giants, who used to see the Twin Towers from their practice field. The following Sunday's NFL games were postponed, and the Giants players abruptly changed their focus.

"Our response was to do something to help," Barber told Giants.com reporter Michael Eisen. "It wasn't anything dramatic that we did. But we showed some support by going down to Ground Zero, and we brought water and supplies. It was an emotional time."

The 9/11 tragedy cast a pall over the entire NFL season, especially for the New York teams. Even on the field, Barber's first few weeks were disappointing. He did little against Kansas City in Week 2 and then pulled a hamstring against New Orleans. He sat out two games, then averaged just 33 yards rushing over his next three outings.

Only in the next four games did Barber start to earn his enormous paycheck. He rushed for 118, 55, 124, and 110 yards. Yet the Giants lost three of those games, dropping their record to 5–7. A nail-biter victory over Seattle on December 23 upped their mark to 7–7 and put the playoffs in reach, but they lost their final two games. After one season of glory, the Giants plummeted back to mediocrity.

Barber rushed for 865 yards and caught 72 passes in a solid but disappointing year. Moreover, Barber's inability to hold onto the ball irritated coaches and fans. He had fumbled nine times (losing three) during the Super Bowl season, and he coughed it up eight times (losing two) in 2001. Barber's fumbling problems would not improve over the next two seasons. At times over this four-year period, fans showered him with boos whenever he dropped the ball. The term "fumbalaya" became associated with Barber. He felt horrible.

While in Chicago one night, a hostile drunk asked Barber why he could not hold onto the ball—lacing the question with

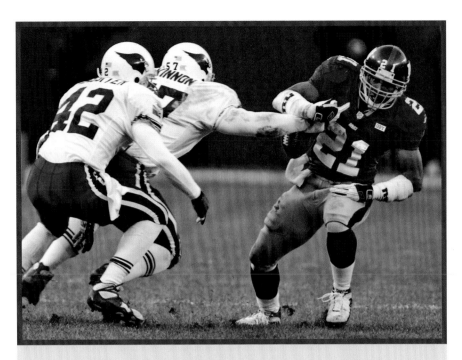

Arizona Cardinals linebacker Ronald McKinnon strips the ball from Tiki Barber during a game on December 15, 2001, at Giants Stadium. Fumbles were becoming a problem for Barber, who coughed up the ball eight times (losing two) during the 2001 season.

obscenities. Tiki instinctively wanted to charge after the guy, but fortunately Ronde and one of their friends, Lep, stepped in. Lep scared off the guy with a frightening look, thus avoiding a potentially ugly scene.

More trouble brewed in March 2002. Teammate Michael Strahan, who had set an NFL record in 2001 with 22½ sacks, turned down a seven-year, $58 million contract offer from the Giants. Included was a $17 million bonus. Barber, loyal to his team's owners and wanting to win in 2002, was upset that Strahan would not accept the deal. "I don't know if he realizes how much $17 million is," Barber told the *New York Post.* "That is absolutely ridiculous, to turn that down."

Barber broke a cardinal rule in sports—criticizing a teammate in the press. The New York media jumped all over the story, pitting one Giants star against the other. Teammate Keith Hamilton responded by ripping Barber in *The Star-Ledger*. "For him to shoot his mouth off, acting like he's Mr. New York, yeah, I'm ticked off," Hamilton said. "Who is Tiki Barber to shoot his mouth off? What has he done? He talks like he's acting in the best interest of the team. Tell him to give his $7 million [signing bonus] back."

Although Barber always believes he has the right to speak his mind, he did regret causing so much friction. Strahan eventually signed with the Giants, and the two went on to have an

LIVING LARGE IN MANHATTAN

It was Ginny Barber, not her famous husband, who wanted to move to the heart of New York City. At first, Tiki harped on Manhattan's many faults. It was dirty, crowded, and ridiculously expensive, he complained. Once he settled in, though, Barber began to dig the New York vibe. He loved the city's energy, excitement, and endless possibilities.

Tiki and Ginny lived in several apartments on the Upper East Side of Manhattan. When they began to think about having their first child, they wondered if they should move to the suburbs. But as they discussed it over dinner at a quaint French bistro in their neighborhood, Tiki came to a revelation: They loved New York too much; they could never leave.

Manhattan, one of the five boroughs of New York City, is the most densely populated area in the United States. Though it is a mere two miles wide and 13 miles long (3.2 kilometers wide and 21 kilometers long), more than 1.5 million people live there. Moreover, great throngs of people flock to the island every business day. Purchased by the amicable relationship. They both shared the same goal in 2002: Get the Giants back to the postseason.

40-YARD DASHES

On July 8, 2002, shortly before training camp began, Ginny gave birth to the couple's first child. They named him Atiim Kiambu—just like his father—but they didn't call him Tiki. Instead, the little fellow goes by A.J., short for Atiim Junior.

Barber says that his children have added joy, meaning, and depth to his life. In 2002, he played like a new man. In the first

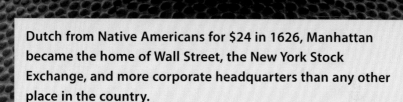

Dutch from Native Americans for $24 in 1626, Manhattan became the home of Wall Street, the New York Stock Exchange, and more corporate headquarters than any other place in the country.

In Manhattan, you will find many of New York's greatest attractions. You can shop at Tiffany's and Saks 5th Avenue or visit such landmarks as Carnegie Hall, Rockefeller Center, and Radio City Music Hall. Manhattan boasts numerous world-class museums as well as Madison Square Garden, the Empire State Building, and the United Nations Headquarters.

The "wealthiest ZIP code" in the United States is on the Upper East Side, where the per-person annual income exceeds $90,000. Many condominiums sell for millions of dollars. For Barber, Manhattan is a lot more affordable now than it was in 1997, when he made a rookie's salary. In his final season with the Giants, he earned $4.5 million, not including millions more in endorsements. For those with money to spend, like Barber, Manhattan is the place to be.

seven games, he did not reach 100 yards rushing. However, he was so effective as a pass-catcher that he surpassed 100 total yards from scrimmage in five of those seven games. Then came the breakout performances.

Against Jacksonville, Barber rushed for 101 yards and scored two touchdowns. One came on a 44-yard scamper—the longest touchdown run by a Giant in more than two years. The next week, he upped his rushing yardage to 127 while also scoring the game-winning touchdown. Trailing Minnesota 20-19 at the noisy Metrodome, Barber barreled in from eight yards out with 2:43 to go. New York won the next game, too, improving its record to 6–4.

Beginning the next week in Houston, Barber accomplished something that had not been achieved since the 1970 merger between the NFL and the American Football League: He ripped off 40-plus-yard rushes in four consecutive games.

The first burst, against the Texans, was the longest. After angling right with the ball, Barber reversed field. Quarterback Kerry Collins helped spring him free with a block. Barber broke a tackle, eluded a diving linebacker, and raced down the left sideline to the Texans' 16. The 70-yard run helped him amass a career-high 146 yards rushing for the day. It also clinched his selection as the NFC Offensive Player of the Month for November.

In the next three games, he broke free for rushes of 42, 43, and 60 yards. The 60-yard explosion came during an electrifying 37-7 rout of Dallas at Giants Stadium. With a 44-27 thumping of Indianapolis the next week, the Giants had a 9–6 record entering the season finale against the Eagles. They needed to win to make the playoffs. It turned into one of the most eventful, and emotional, games in Tiki Barber's life.

A GAMUT OF EMOTIONS

Facing one of the toughest defenses in the NFL, coach Jim Fassel put the ball in Barber's hands. He took 32 handoffs.

Tiki Barber runs down the sideline for a gain of 70 yards on November 24, 2002, as Houston Texan defenders *(from left)* Matt Stevens, Jeff Posey, and Marcus Coleman try to catch him. In four straight games in 2002, Barber had runs of 40 yards or more.

He rushed for 203 yards. And he fumbled the ball away three times. The Giants would outgain Philadelphia 461 to 209, but Barber's fumbles were killer. His **turnover** at New York's 26-yard line with 4:34 left in the fourth quarter nearly cost the Giants the game. At the end of regulation, it was 7-7.

By overtime, even the coaches wondered if Barber should be yanked from the field—except for the head coach. "Everyone was asking me if we should get [Ron] Dayne in," Fassel said after the game, "and I said, nope, [Barber] is the guy who got us here; he's the guy who's going to stay in and win it with us."

In overtime, Barber gained 28 yards on four touches, putting New York on the Eagles' 20-yard line. Fans clutched their hearts when Barber and quarterback Kerry Collins botched the next handoff, but Barber recovered. Matt Bryant then booted a 39-yard field goal to send the Giants to the playoffs.

"The gamut of emotions that I ran through today was unbelievable," Barber said afterward. "I told Matt Bryant after he kicked that field goal that it takes a lot to make me cry, but when that thing went through, I couldn't help myself. As much as I did, running the ball and what not, it is the fumbles that will stick with me. Fortunately, we got away with this one, but it is something that we have to correct, and I know it's all on me."

After the game, Barber hugged Fassel and said, "Coach, thanks for sticking with me." "I told him that it wasn't a hard call for me," Fassel said. "I love the young man. He's won a lot of games for me, I've stuck by him before, and I'll stick by him again."

Only statistically was Barber second-best. Both his 203 yards rushing and 276 all-purpose yards (he caught eight passes for 73 yards) were the second-best single-game totals ever for a Giant. He finished the season with 1,387 rushing yards (second most ever for a Giant at the time) and 9,069 career total yards—No. 2 in team annals behind Frank Gifford's 9,862.

The Giants' emotional roller-coaster ride crashed and burned in the opening playoff game. Facing the 49ers in San Francisco, Barber rushed for 115 yards and totaled 62 yards on receptions. After he scored in the third quarter to put the Giants up 35-14, he blew a kiss to the opposing fans. A field goal made it 38-14 with 19:27 left in the game.

Shockingly, quarterback Jeff Garcia rallied the Niners, putting 25 points on the board to take a 39-38 lead. The desperate Giants tried a 41-yard field goal as time expired, but they botched the snap and hold. Holder Matt Allen attempted a desperation pass. And although a defender was guilty of **pass interference** (according to Mike Pereira, the NFL supervisor of officials), no flag was thrown.

In sum, Tiki blew a kiss, the refs blew the call, and the Giants blew the game. Four weeks later, Barber went to San Diego to watch his brother play in the Super Bowl.

Overcoming Fumble-itis

Ever wonder what an NFL running back eats for breakfast? Before the 2003 season, *Men's Fitness* magazine posed that question to Tiki Barber. The Giants star had motored downfield for nearly 2,000 total yards the year before. How did he keep his engine running?

Not with fast foods, that's for sure. "I maintain a high-fiber, low-carb, low-fat diet," Barber revealed in the magazine. "I have slightly elevated cholesterol, so on a typical morning I'll have a V8 with Fiber One cereal mixed with Smart Start cereal so it tastes a little sweet. I get basically three-quarters the amount of fiber I need in one sitting."

Hamburgers and fries for lunch? Hardly. Instead, Barber said he often ate a spinach salad with pears, tofu, balsamic dressing, and just a little bacon for flavor. Or sometimes he would eat a tuna fish or turkey sandwich—on whole-wheat bread, of course. He would load up on protein at dinnertime, usually eating chicken or steak.

Barber did alter his diet prior to game days. If the game were on a Sunday, he would consume large helpings of carbohydrates on Friday—including lots of bread and pasta. On Saturday, he would chug a large protein shake.

What Barber did not care for was the food at the Giants' training table. He did like their homemade waffles, but those were available only upon request. "The worst food is the spaghetti," he told *Men's Fitness*. "It's like soggy worms—not even close to *al dente*. I live in New York, where the pasta is phenomenal. I don't eat spaghetti that looks like it was made by a five-year-old."

At age 28, Barber entered the 2003 training camp physically fit and optimistic about the new season. The Giants hoped to build on their strong 2002 finish and make the playoffs once again. Nothing happened on Week 1 to change their minds.

DOWNWARD SPIRAL

In the opening game, New York hosted a potent St. Louis Rams team. The Giants defense stuck it to the Rams, forcing four turnovers and knocking quarterback Kurt Warner from the game. All the while, Barber ripped off big gains. In the second quarter, his back-to-back runs of 15 and 22 yards set up a touchdown. New York won 23-13 as Barber rushed for 146 yards. At the time, it was the third-highest total of his career.

The next week, the Giants hosted one of most dramatic games in the history of *Monday Night Football*. Down 29-14 to Dallas early in the fourth quarter, Giants quarterback Kerry Collins spearheaded a furious comeback. With less than seven minutes to play, wide receiver Amani Toomer made a juggling catch in the end zone to cut the lead to 29-27. New York tried to tie the game with a **two-point conversion**. After two

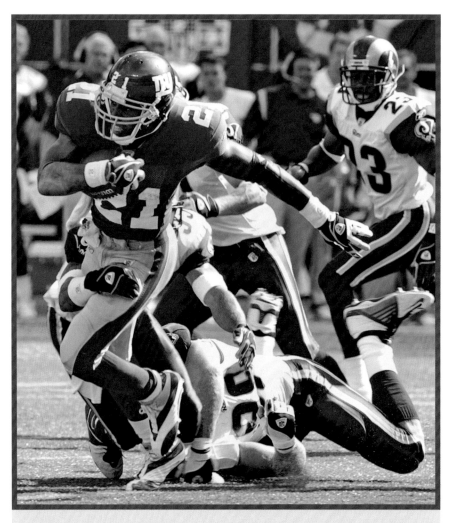

Tiki Barber gains 11 yards during a fourth-quarter run against the St. Louis Rams on Opening Day in 2003. Barber had 24 carries for 146 yards, and the Giants won 23-13. The game would be one of the few highlights for the Giants during the 2003 season.

pass-interference penalties on Dallas, Barber plunged into the end zone to make it 29-29.

Late in the fourth quarter, Barber's heroics in the red zone seemed to seal the Cowboys' fate. He earned a first down with a tough three-yard run up the middle, then bulled through the defense for five more yards. With 11 seconds left, kicker Matt Bryant booted a 30-yard field goal for an apparent 32-29 victory.

Dallas, though, would not die. Bryant squibbed the kick-off out of bounds, giving the Cowboys the ball at their own 40-yard line. After a 26-yard pass from Quincy Carter to Antonio Bryant, the Cowboys had the ball on the Giants' 34. Kicker Billy Cundiff then blasted a 52-yard field goal—the longest of his career—to tie the score. Dallas won in overtime, 35-32, on Cundiff's NFL record-tying seventh field goal of the game. "That is a tough one," Giants coach Jim Fassel said after the game. "I thought both teams played their guts out."

The loss was a bad omen for the Giants. The next week, they blew an 18-point lead at Washington before surviving with a 24-21 overtime win. Barber rushed for 126 yards. But over the next three weeks, Barber and the offense fell flat as the Giants lost each game. After wins against Minnesota and the rival New York Jets (also in overtime), the bottom fell out. The Giants lost their final eight games of the season. They finished at 4–12, tying them with Arizona, San Diego, and Oakland for the worst record in the NFL.

Barber rushed for 120 yards in Week 10 and 111 yards on the following Sunday. But over the last six games, he averaged just 12 carries and 50 yards per outing. The offense was abysmal during the eight-game losing streak, averaging just 9.8 points per game.

Despite weekly disappointments, Barber tried to maintain a positive attitude. "All these fans that I see around, I tell them, these bad times make the good times better," he told reporters. "That's what we look for, that's what we think about."

The losing got so bad that, with two weeks to go, head coach Jim Fassel asked management if it planned to fire him. He requested that, if the team was going to do so, please do it before the season ended. The Giants granted his wish. They also allowed him to coach until the season's end.

Following the final game, players and fans showered Fassel with love and praise. The long-respected coach had gone 58–45–1 for New York before the eight-game skid. Barber, whose rookie season in 1997 was Fassel's first as a head coach, had only praise for his one and only NFL coach. "This year has been an anomaly," Barber said, as reported on Giants.com. "But otherwise, he's taken some teams that didn't have a lot of talent and took them pretty far. He [deserves] a lot of credit."

Despite the dismal season, Barber still produced outstanding numbers. His 1,216 rushing yards ranked fifth in the NFC, as did his 1,677 yards from scrimmage. He also became the first Giant to lead the team in both receptions (69) and rushing yards in the same season since Joe Dawkins in 1974. Moreover, he finished the season as New York's all-time leader in total yards (10,746) and receptions (422).

Proving himself a playmaker, Barber ranked third in the NFC with 92 first downs. On the down side, he scored only three touchdowns because Fassel was afraid to give him the ball near the goal line. Barber was still suffering from fumble-itis. He had lost six fumbles in 2002 and a half-dozen more in 2003. Fassel's successor would need to help Barber cure this dreaded disease.

NEW AND IMPROVED

On January 6, 2004, the Giants hired taskmaster Tom Coughlin as their new head coach. In contrast to Barber's perpetual beaming smile, Coughlin usually wore a grim expression. He had coached football since before Barber was born, and he had been an assistant under the legendary Bill Parcells when the Giants won Super Bowl XXV in January 1991. More impressive, as head coach of Jacksonville, he took the Jaguars to the playoffs in four of their first five NFL seasons.

Besides welcoming his second NFL coach in early 2004, Barber also became a father for the second time. On March 18,

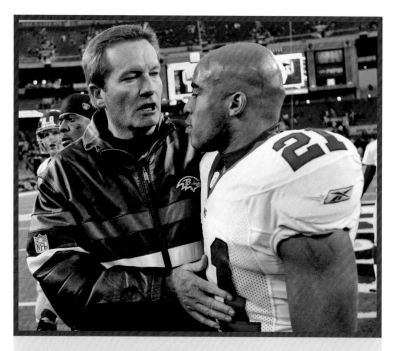

With two games left in the 2003 campaign, the Giants informed coach Jim Fassel that he would be let go after the season. Tiki Barber always had praise for Fassel, who joined the Giants the same year that Barber did. Here, the two share words after a Giants-Ravens game in 2004—Fassel had become Baltimore's offensive coordinator.

2004, Ginny gave birth to Chason Cole. Tiki treasured the next few months at home with the new baby, for he knew a rigorous training camp lay ahead.

High on Coughlin's to-do list was to teach Barber how to hold onto the ball. Coughlin and running backs coach Jerald Ingram knew that Barber's slippery grip had deflated the Giants' offense at times.

"He got to the point where he became a marked man," Ingram told the *Sporting News*. "Defenses were coming after him saying, 'Hey, we're going after the ball. As fast as you can, get the hands on the ball; don't worry about tackling him, tackle the ball.'"

Barber recalled a meeting with Coughlin in the spring of 2004. The new coach did not mince words. "Before minicamp, Coach Coughlin called me in," Barber recounted in *Sports*

A SPEECH OF PASSION

When Virginia's Class of 2004 was asked to pick its valediction speaker, it chose former Cavaliers running back Tiki Barber. Of course, this football player was no "dumb jock." At the outdoor Valediction Exercises on May 15, 2004, Barber delivered a thoughtful, stirring speech that was as motivational as any halftime pep talk.

Barber aimed to inspire the young women and men who were about to embark on their careers. First, he recognized how hard it is for a person to decide what to do with his or her life. "I've been playing football for eight years now," he said, "and I still don't know what I want to be when I grow up." But the even tougher question, he said, is *Why?* "This is your internal reason for doing things," he said. "It's not what you tell other people; it's what you tell yourself."

Barber told the story of his brutal two-and-a-half-mile climbs uphill in the dead of winter. It was during these lonely moments that he discovered his *why*. He realized that he did not want to be average but better than average. Though his muscles ached and the cold wind battered his face, he realized he was bettering himself with each agonizing step—and he loved it. "And I would encourage all of you," he said, "as you make choices to figure out what you want to do, to find your passion."

Barber stressed how it took hard work, dedication, and sacrifice to reach one's goals. He also talked about heroism,

Illustrated. "It was like being called to the principal's office. I walk in, and he says, 'You have talent, but your turnovers hurt the team. I want you to change how you carry the ball. I want

personified by former NFL star Pat Tillman, who had quit football to fight in the war against terrorism. On April 22, 2004, he was killed in action in Afghanistan. Barber described Tillman as "someone who display[ed] courage, nobility, and strength in the face of opposition."

Barber added that men and women did not have to fight to prove their heroism. "[A]nother definition that I think is more applicable to most of us is someone who fights for a cause," he said. "[S]omewhere along the line you'll find out there's a greater calling for you. There are so many ills in our society, whether it's poverty, AIDS, illiteracy, drug abuse, domestic violence, or in some subtle and not so subtle ways, racism."

Barber told the students that they had three choices: "You can turn a blind eye; you can lend your support from arm's length; or you can embrace it with conviction, and that's what I encourage all of you to do. The principles and the ideals that you use to be successful in business are the exact same ones that you can use to help a starving family, the same ones that can provide support for someone afflicted with a disease. It's the same inspiration that will give a battered woman the strength to walk out and fight for her life."

Amid heartfelt applause, Barber left the podium. He had delivered a message of passion and compassion. With his advice, Barber hoped, the world would be a better place due to the Class of 2004.

you to hold it high and tight, and I want you to always be cognizant of it.' And that was it. It was blunt, it was honest. I was really appreciative of how he handled it."

Coughlin's Jaguars had been exceptional at avoiding turnovers, and Coughlin and Ingram taught Barber the secrets of ball security. Previously, Barber had held the ball horizontally with his elbow out. His coaches told him to hold it vertically with his elbow in. Barber obliged, cradling it that way not just during plays but during team drills and while running on the treadmill. Remember, Ingram told Barber, as recounted in *Sports Illustrated*, "The ball is your friend."

Barber might not have realized it, but Ingram was helping to transform him into a superstar. Besides fixing the fumble problem, he addressed Barber's physical strength. Recalled Barber in *Sports Illustrated*: "My first meeting with him, his first question was, 'How strong are you?' I was like, 'I don't know. I don't really work out upper body.' Ingram told me I needed to get stronger."

For a couple of seasons, Barber had trained by boxing. The sessions were great cardiovascular workouts, but they did not improve his strength. After talking with Ingram, Barber began to work with Joe Carini, who had won New Jersey's Strongest Man competition six straight years in the 1980s.

With four intense sessions per week, Barber became incrementally stronger. In the summer of 2005, *Sports Illustrated* would report that he was leg pressing 950 pounds (431 kilograms) and dead-lifting 400 pounds (181 kilograms) over his head. In one routine, Barber carried 400 pounds on his shoulders for 20 yards (18 meters)—which made clingy linebackers feel like rag dolls.

The transformation of Tiki Barber did not end there. Ingram worked with him to improve his mental approach to the game. "Everything in sports is half physical, half mental," Barber told the *Sporting News*. "That was the big focus this year. 'Tiki, you've got to find a way to play above the X's and O's, play above the regular call of duty.' It's helped a ton."

By the first game of the 2004 season, Barber was stronger, more focused, and no longer concerned about fumbling the ball. He was about to begin the first **Pro Bowl** season of his NFL career.

UNSTOPPABLE

Early in the season, Coughlin looked like a miracle worker. New York lost its opening game, 31-17, to a powerful Eagles team, but the new and improved Barber looked spectacular. He rushed for 125 yards on just nine carries, including a 72-yard touchdown romp in the fourth quarter. He also caught five passes for 75 yards, giving him 200 yards for the afternoon. "I think we're much better off than we were last year," Barber said afterward. "We did a lot of good things, and that's encouraging. We just have to keep building on it."

That they did. Over the next four weeks, the Giants knocked off Washington, Cleveland, Green Bay, and Dallas. In the last three of those games, Barber carried the ball exactly 23 times each game. The results: 106, 182, and 122 yards rushing. Against the Packers and the Cowboys, he amassed nearly 200 yards from scrimmage (rushing and receiving) each game.

Coughlin's complex offense helped Barber flourish. The coach ran multiple plays from the same formation, making it difficult for defenses to key on Barber. Moreover, Coughlin and Ingram helped cure Barber of his fumbling malady. He would cough up the ball only twice all season. With the Giants now able to trust his hands, he got to carry the ball in the red zone. He would score 15 touchdowns on the season—a career high and a dozen more than in 2003.

In addition, Barber's improved physical and mental strength was paying dividends. His days as a jitterbug back were long behind him. He didn't just avoid tacklers; he bashed into defenders, often breaking tackles or carrying men a yard or two downfield.

Facing the Green Bay Packers in October 2004, Tiki Barber breaks away for a 52-yard touchdown in the third quarter. He piled up 182 rushing yards against the Packers. Barber had worked in the off-season with running backs coach Jerald Ingram on strength training and on reducing his number of fumbles.

Some credited New York's 4–1 start to quarterback Kurt Warner. A former Pro Bowl/Super Bowl quarterback with the St. Louis Rams, Warner had fallen on hard times in recent seasons before re-emerging with the Giants in 2004. Most of the cheers, however, rained on Barber. Through the first five games, he had accumulated 817 yards from scrimmage. In the history of the NFL, only legends Jim Brown and O.J. Simpson had amassed higher totals through five contests.

After getting Week 6 off, the Giants hoped to be stronger than ever for their next game. It didn't happen. New York lost

28-13 at home to the Detroit Lions, a team notorious for its ineptness on the road. Barber still shone, rushing for 70 yards and tallying 102 reception yards. The Giants rolled the next week, 34-13 at Minnesota, as Barber ran for 101 yards and two touchdowns.

During the season, Barber impressed upon his young teammates the urgency of winning a Super Bowl. Players' careers are short, he said, and the opportunity to win it all is rare. With New York now 5–2, Barber and Giants fans thought this could be the year.

But incredibly, the nightmare of 2003 returned. Once again, New York lost eight games in a row. The first two losses were close, but with Kurt Warner struggling, coach Coughlin replaced him with Eli Manning. The much-celebrated rookie was the son of legendary New Orleans quarterback Archie Manning. He was also the kid brother of Indianapolis quarterback Peyton Manning (who won the NFL MVP Award in 2003 and 2004).

The Giants hoped that the Manning magic would rub off on them, but it wasn't to be. They lost to Atlanta 14-10 before getting blown out by their East Coast neighbors: Philadelphia, Washington, and Baltimore. Next came a 33-30 loss to a Pittsburgh team that had won 11 games in a row. Finally, a series of Giants breakdowns in the last 2:19 of the game allowed Cincinnati to overtake them 23-22.

Throughout the eight-game ordeal, Barber remained a steady force. He rushed for 107 yards against Atlanta, 108 versus Arizona, 109 against the Bengals, and 110 versus the Eagles. His succession of 100-yard rushing games gave him nine for the season—a new team record. Entering the last game of the season against Dallas, stat freaks closely examined his numbers.

They discovered that, if Barber could rush for 65 yards against the Cowboys, he would tie the Giants' career rushing record of 6,897 yards held by Rodney Hampton. Moreover, if he could somehow muster 93 rushing yards, he would equal the Giants' season mark of 1,516 yards set by little Joe Morris in 1986.

THE RECORDS FALL

In the season finale at Giants Stadium, Barber steadily built his rushing totals through the first 40-plus minutes. Then, on the final play of the third quarter, he broke Hampton's career record with a four-yard run. But when Dallas took a 24-21 lead with 1:49 remaining, the season record as well as the game seemed hopelessly out of reach. Manning had lost all six of his starts, and few had faith that he could play Captain Comeback in the last 109 seconds. But he did have one secret weapon: Tiki Barber.

Manning began the drive with a 23-yard pass play to his star running back. After a penalty, New York had the ball on the Cowboys' 28. Barber still needed 21 yards to tie Morris's season rushing record, but he picked up 10 of those on the next play. After a five-yard pass to Marcellus Rivers, Barber gained 10 yards on a pair of runs. With the ball on the 3-yard line, the Giants called their final timeout with 16 seconds left. Adding to the drama, Barber was just one yard short of Morris's record.

Everyone expected a pass play, because if the pass were incomplete the clock would stop. That would give the Giants one or two more plays to score a touchdown or kick the field goal. If they ran the ball and did not score, the clock could run out before they had a chance for another play.

So what play did Coughlin call? Tiki Barber up the middle.

Before the game, Giants center Shaun O'Hara had asked Barber, "Are you ready for a storybook ending?" O'Hara could never have imagined this chain of events. With the Cowboys looking for the pass, Manning handed the ball to Barber, who simply plunged up the middle and into the end zone. The crowd went wild. The extra point secured a 28-24 victory. It

David Tyree lifts Tiki Barber after Barber scored the game-winning touch-down against the Dallas Cowboys on January 2, 2005. With the touchdown, Barber broke the Giants' record for most rushing yards in a season. Earlier in the game, he broke the Giants' career rushing record.

was the latest in a game that the Giants had come from behind to win since 1953.

"Unbelievable," O'Hara raved after the game. "Tiki is awe-some, and he makes everybody around him better. I am just glad to be a part of him and the Giants."

"It's phenomenal," Barber said in the postgame news con-ference. About his record-breaking performance, he said, "It justifies everything that I have done—in the off-season and the meticulous attention to detail that I have tried to correct my problems and my faults. To have everything go the way it did today, it's amazing."

Barber not only bettered Hampton's and Morris's records, but he also broke one of his own. His 2,096 all-purpose yards (rushing, receptions, returns) broke his own team record of 2,085 set in 2000. Those 2,096 yards all came from scrimmage (meaning none on returns), and they were the most yards from scrimmage in the NFL that season.

Barber's 1,518 rushing yards ranked fifth in the NFL—and second in the NFC behind Shaun Alexander's 1,696. In Pro Bowl balloting, NFL coaches, players, and fans voted in Barber for the first time. Many say that the Pro Bowl game, staged in Honolulu every February, does not mean much. But it meant a lot to a pair of NFC players. For the first time since college, twin brothers Tiki and Ronde were teammates once again.

Finishing
with a Bang

At the Pro Bowl in February 2005, as he basked in the Hawaiian sunshine, Tiki Barber must have wondered, *Could it get any better than this?* Incredibly, it would. After smashing the 2,000-total-yard barrier in 2004, Barber would compile even more yardage in the following season. But even before that, he would visit with one of the most famous political leaders in the world.

In March 2005, Barber, his wife, and their friends dined at the restaurant Tao in New York. During dinner, a man approached Barber and, as recounted in *New York* magazine, said, "Shimon Peres would like to meet you."

Peres was the former prime minister of Israel and the winner of the 1994 Nobel Peace Prize. Barber could not believe that the revered leader wanted to meet him, but he did not shy away. Barber walked over and said hello.

"My people tell me you're the best," Peres told Barber. "You know," he replied, "I'm pretty good."

The two chatted for about 10 minutes before Peres gave Barber his card. "You should come see my country," Peres said. "I'd love to!" Barber replied.

A few weeks later, Barber called the former prime minister's office and said he was on his way. The Barbers flew to Israel in June, and while in Tel Aviv, they stayed at the Dan Hotel. Their room, they were told, was the same one that President Bill Clinton had stayed in. The Barbers toured the holy city of Jerusalem and visited the Knesset, Israel's parliament. They also went to the lowest point on Earth, the Dead Sea. That body of water is so laden with salt that even muscle-bound football players like Barber have no trouble floating on it.

Barber also got a sense of the Israeli-Palestinian conflict that has made international headlines for 60 years. "There was a protest where they threw tar and nails onto a highway and backed up traffic," Barber said. "We were there—we were right in the middle of it." More than ever, Barber knew that he wanted more out of life than football. It would not be long before he himself would report on important news events.

30 YEARS YOUNG

On April 7, 2005, Barber turned 30—old age for a running back—but he reported to training camp in prime condition. Moreover, reporters observed the sharpness of his cuts and routes. In early September, the Giants rewarded their most valuable player with a contract extension. His existing pact was due to expire after the 2006 season, but the new contract would guarantee him a salary through the 2008 campaign (provided that he did not voluntarily retire). The extension brought his salary in line with other top running backs.

Shimon Peres, the former prime minister of Israel, welcomes Tiki Barber to his office in Tel Aviv in June 2005. Barber toured Jerusalem and was able to get a sense of the Israeli-Palestinian conflict. He was beginning to think more and more about his life outside of football.

In 2005, the Giants expected a much more potent offense. In addition to the maturity of quarterback Eli Manning, they added Plaxico Burress, a big-play receiver who had compiled 1,325 yards receiving with Pittsburgh in 2002. Thanks partly to a soft early-season schedule, New York started 3–1 while averaging 34 points a game.

One victory came at the expense of beleaguered New Orleans. The Saints had to move their scheduled home game against New York to Giants Stadium because of the recent hurricane (Katrina) in Louisiana. The Saints wore their home uniforms, but that did not mean a thing. The Giants routed them 27-10, with Barber rushing for 83 yards and scoring two touchdowns. Barber ran for 128 yards against St. Louis in Week 4, and on October 25 the Giants were sitting pretty at 4–2. What followed was one of the most emotional weeks in the history of the franchise—and of Tiki Barber's lifetime.

A WIN FOR MR. MARA

As a youngster, Wellington Mara served as a ballboy for the New York Giants, which his father, Tim, had purchased in 1925. Wellington inherited the team in 1959, and he became one of the most beloved owners in all of sports. Mara cared deeply for his players, especially if they suffered personal crises. When he died on Tuesday, October 25, 2005, at age 89, the Giants and their fans mourned his loss.

Barber, who was particularly close to Mara, visited him at his home the day before he died. Giants players were among the 2,000 people who attended his funeral Mass on Friday at St. Patrick's Cathedral in New York. At Giants Stadium on Sunday, while wearing "W.T.M." patches on their jerseys, the Giants vowed to win one for Mr. Mara.

Barber displayed particular passion after promising that he would score a touchdown in honor of the revered owner. From the opening kickoff against Washington, Barber was nearly unstoppable. On his first carry, he raced around the left end and sprinted 57 yards.

"That's exactly how he [Mara] would have preferred it," said his son, John, in *USA Today.* "If he said it once, he said it a hundred times: 'Run the ball, run the ball.'"

Barber kept on running. On another rushing play, he romped 59 yards, achieving the extremely rare NFL feat of two 50-yard runs in the same game. Then, with 1:07 left in the third quarter, Barber busted in from four yards out for his first touchdown. Amid the raucous cheers, Barber trotted to

Tiki Barber breaks free from the grasp of the Redskins' Pierson Prioleau to score a touchdown on October 30, 2005, at Giants Stadium. A patch with the initials "W.T.M.," seen on Barber's left shoulder, honored Giants owner Wellington Mara, who had died earlier that week at age 89. The Giants had vowed to win one for Mara, and Barber rushed for a career-high 206 yards, as New York throttled Washington 36–0.

the sideline and presented the ball to Tim McDonnell, one of Mara's 40 grandchildren.

"This is for you," Barber told him, as reported in *USA Today*. "This is for your grandpa."

Barber enjoyed the game of his life, rushing 24 times for a career-high 206 yards. The Giants not only scored 36 points, but they also recorded their first regular-season shutout in seven years. In fact, Redskins coach Joe Gibbs was blanked for the first time in his 207 games as an NFL bench boss.

RUNNING WILD

After the emotional Washington game, Barber ran for 71, 95, and 112 yards in his next three contests. In his remaining six games, he was a runaway locomotive, averaging 149 yards per game. To understand what a phenomenal accomplishment that was, consider this: When Eric Dickerson set the (still-standing) NFL record for rushing yards in a season in 1984, he averaged *132* yards per game.

Against the 8–2 Seattle Seahawks, Barber rushed for 151 yards. If only he could have kicked, too. With the score tied 21-21, Giants **placekicker** Jay Feely missed three field goals, and Seattle prevailed 24-21. Barber followed with games of 115 and 124 yards before an epic performance against Kansas City on December 17.

With New York's offensive line banged up, Barber had to earn his yardage. That he did, on one play breaking at least five tackles in a 41-yard touchdown run. On 29 carries, he averaged nearly eight yards a crack. With less than 3:00 to play and the Giants up 20-17, Barber busted off right tackle for a 20-yard touchdown romp. He finished the day with 220 yards, eclipsing Gene "Choo Choo" Roberts's team record of 218 yards set against the long-forgotten Chicago Cardinals in 1950.

Instead of boasting of his accomplishment, Barber praised the overachieving efforts of his offensive line. With both starting tackles hurt, David Diehl (normally a guard) and veteran reserve Bob Whitfield filled in admirably. Rich Seubert started his first game at guard since suffering a broken leg in October 2003.

"Our line took great pride in [the rushing record]," Barber said after the game. "It's something I'm very proud of, and I think it's something that we'll remember for a long time."

It was truly a game for the ages, as Barber established multiple records. He broke the Giants' single-season rushing record, usurping his previous mark of 1,518 set a year earlier.

His two rushing touchdowns upped his career total to 49, tied for tops on the Giants' all-time list with Rodney Hampton. He also broke Hampton's team record of 1,824 carries, and his fifth consecutive 100-yard game set another club record.

In a Christmas Eve loss at Washington the following week, Barber rushed for 80 yards on 16 carries. When Minnesota lost the next day, the Giants clinched a playoff berth.

That was not good enough for Barber, who helped New York clinch the NFC East on New Year's Eve with 203 yards rushing against Oakland. Not only did he become the third man ever to have three 200-yard games in one season, but he also set another Giants record with a 95-yard run. With New York on its own 5-yard line in the first quarter, Barber busted up the middle and kept on going. A key downfield block by wide receiver Plaxico Burress removed his last roadblock to the end zone. The coast-to-coast sprint broke Hap Moran's 75-year-old team record of 91 yards.

Barber's season-ending statistics were astounding. He had rushed a team-record 357 times for 1,860 yards. Although Seattle's Shaun Alexander led the league in rushing in 2005, Barber's 2,390 total yards (rushing and receiving) were the second most in the history of the league. Few other backs in NFL history have had the power, speed, quickness, and hands to do what he did. In fact, he became the first player ever with 1,800 yards rushing and 500 yards receiving in the same year.

Most of the NFL's legendary running backs—from Jim Brown to Barry Sanders to Alexander—established their greatness in their first or second season in the league. Tiki Barber was unique. It took him four years to become a regular starter—and two more to join the NFL's elite. Through sheer hard work, he took his game to higher and higher levels. Though Alexander won the NFL MVP Award in 2005, *Sports Illustrated* honored Barber as its NFL Player of the Year.

TIKI'S TIFF

As a division winner, New York hosted the Carolina Panthers in the NFC wild-card game. Though both teams had finished 11–5, the Panthers surprisingly dominated the Giants. They prevailed 23-0, becoming the first team to record a playoff shutout on the road in 25 years. The Panthers held the ball for 42:45 compared with 17:15 for New York.

"One of the keys to the game was eliminating the big plays and to always have our eyes on Tiki," Panthers defensive end Julius Peppers said after the game. Carolina, which fielded one of the best defenses in the NFL, held Barber to just 41 yards rushing.

Afterward, Barber vented. "They attacked our schemes, they attacked our tendencies, and it was frustrating," he said, as reported by *USA Today*. "They kept a safety in the **box**, and we couldn't exploit it. It was a testament to the fact that our game plan wasn't the greatest one." Several times during his career, Barber sparked controversy by questioning his teammates and coaches—including after this game. In fact, he stated bluntly, "I think in some ways we were outcoached."

Those words angered Giants head coach Tom Coughlin, and the story made headlines in the New York-area papers. On the morning after the game, though, the two men reached a truce. Coughlin showed Barber film of the game and explained how players did not take advantage of certain opportunities.

Afterward, Barber admitted that his comments were probably out of line. "[L]ooking at the tape, it was mostly us not performing as players," he said, according to *The New York Times*. "We had a good conversation," Coughlin told the press. "It is always a good conversation with Tiki. He is a very positive guy. His attitude is great. He said something hopefully he regretted."

That last comment seemed to be a bit of a jab at Barber. Tensions between Coughlin and his star player would continue into the next season—and even after Barber's retirement.

WHEN TIKI MET CONDI

After the playoff blowout, the Pro Bowl turned out to be a washout for Barber. Rain in Honolulu fell hard in the first quarter, and Barber committed a fumble. In 11 carries, he rushed for just 33 yards.

In 2006, more than ever before, Barber contemplated his life after football. He was 31 years old, his body was wearing down, and so many other things in life intrigued him. In April, he even became involved in the national political scene.

Janine Zacharia, a reporter for Bloomberg News, invited Barber to the White House Correspondents' Association Dinner. She believed that U.S. Secretary of State Condoleezza Rice, a huge football fan, would like to meet the cerebral All-Pro running back. Barber attended the event with more than 100 other guests. The eclectic guest list included the Reverend Jesse Jackson, *Jeopardy!* host Alex Trebek, former Los Angeles Dodgers manager Tommy Lasorda, and Prince Turki al-Faisal Al-Saud of Saudi Arabia.

Rice, as Zacharia had predicted, was especially intrigued with Barber. In fact, she even invited him to lunch at the State Department. Not one to shy from the spotlight, Barber said yes. "Within 30 seconds, I feel like I've known her forever," Barber told *The New Yorker.* "She's welcoming and warm. There's no facade."

According to the Washington gossip site Wonkette.com, Barber, Rice, and six others lunched on balsamic glazed sirloin atop arugula salad. The site stated that Rice and Barber discussed the 2006 NFL Draft. Rice wondered why the Houston Texans passed on drafting Heisman Trophy winner Reggie Bush. Reportedly, she expressed her approval of the free agents that her favorite team, the Cleveland Browns, had signed.

"I asked her if she wanted to be NFL commissioner," Barber recalled in *The New Yorker.* He said she responded: "Oh, I'd love to, but I got to figure out Iran first." Barber beamed his trademark smile. "She's a phenomenal, phenomenal lady," he said.

MAN OF MANY MEDIUMS

By the time he rubbed elbows with Condoleezza Rice, Barber was already a household name in the United States. He had become a media darling. To advertisers, he had a complete package of charms: athletic stardom, intelligence, rugged good looks, an eye-catching smile, glowing self-confidence, and a down-to-earth personality. Women found him attractive, and men admired his athleticism and character. It helped, too, that he starred on the biggest of stages—New York.

Barber's crossover appeal was reflected in the shoes he sponsored. He served as a spokesman not only for Foot Locker and Reebok (sneakers for young athletes), but also for Johnston and Murphy—dress shoes and apparel for men. For one of Johnston and Murphy's ads, he dressed in a sophisticated suit while leaning on a football that rested on the arm of a leather couch.

The man who hates to be pigeonholed has done commercials for both McDonald's (inexpensive fast food) and Cadillac (luxury vehicles). His Dish Network commercial, in which he and a cable guy go bonkers over the number of football games they are getting on the dish, was hilarious. He has also done ads for PowerBar, Steiner Sports Memorabilia, and Audemars Piguet—a luxury Swiss watchmaker. In an ad for the Visa Check Card, Tiki and Ronde confuse a sales clerk who doesn't know whose name matches the card.

Tiki has overcome obstacles so remarkably that he has become a sought-after motivational speaker, earning $40,000 a speech. In 2006, he hosted a show on Sirius Satellite Radio called *The National Sweep,* in which he discussed news, politics, sports, and entertainment. His guests included U.S. Senator John McCain and Daniel Kurtzer, the former ambassador to both Israel and Egypt. In 2007, Tiki and Ronde's *The Barber Shop* was still going strong on Sirius Satellite Radio. During the football season, it aired on Tuesdays at 7:00 P.M. Well before joining *Today,* he worked as a correspondent on *Fox & Friends,* a Fox News Channel morning show.

In addition, Tiki has contributed his time and money to numerous charities. He has been involved in Meals on Wheels, the Muscular Dystrophy Association, UNICEF, and Learning Leaders and in the fight against pediatric AIDS. Moreover, he has contributed to DARE, the Starlight Foundation, and the Ronald McDonald House. He has also teamed with Colgate-Palmolive to unveil the U.S. Surgeon General's Seven Steps to a Bright Smile.

In recent years, Barber has shown off his writing talents. Beginning in 2004, he and Ronde co-wrote four inspirational children's books about their days in youth football. The success of the first book, *By My Brother's Side,* inspired *Game Day, Teammates,* and *Kickoff!* In September 2007, Simon & Schuster published his memoir, *Tiki: My Life in the Game and Beyond.* Barber acknowledged that it was unusual for a 32-year-old to write a memoir, but few people have experienced so much in so little time.

To top it all off, Barber made the International Best Dressed List (it helps to have a fashion-conscious wife) in 2007 and was featured in *People's* 2006 "Sexiest Man Alive" issue. The magazine profiled Tiki and Ronde together under the category "Doubly Delicious." Once again, the twins were inseparable.

PONDERING RETIREMENT

When he arrived in training camp in the summer of 2006, Barber dropped hints that he would not remain in the NFL for long. According to *Washington Post* sports columnist Mark Maske, "Barber talked at length about the possibility of retiring within the next few years to pursue his off-field interests in broadcasting and business."

In the season's first few games, Barber ran well but was not the unstoppable force of late 2005. In the opening game, he rushed for 110 yards but was hardly the focus of attention. In this game, the first Sunday night matchup ever on NBC,

Tiki Barber and his wife, Ginny Cha, pose for photographers before attending the Fresh Air Fund Benefit Gala in June 2007 in New York City. Barber has been involved in numerous charities, including Meals on Wheels, UNICEF, DARE, and the Ronald McDonald House. In 2006, he and his brother, Ronde, donated $1 million to their alma mater, the University of Virginia.

brothers Peyton and Eli Manning faced each other as the respective quarterbacks of Indianapolis and New York.

The next two weeks, Philadelphia and Seattle held Barber in check, but he rushed for 123 yards in his subsequent outing against Washington. The next week, Barber dominated the headlines. First came his virtuoso performance against Atlanta. The Falcons entered the game ranked second in the NFL in rushing defense, but Barber marched downfield like a Sherman tank. He amassed 185 yards rushing, including nine runs of at least 12 yards. After the game, Falcons running back Warrick Dunn said, "They just ran it down our throats."

The bigger news came later in the week. Barber told *The New York Times* that he was "leaning toward" retiring after the 2006 season and that he had "pretty much" made up his mind to do so. That admission sent shockwaves around the NFL. Few superstars in any sport had ever walked away at the peak of their careers.

Immediately, critics attacked Barber's decision. Commentators and columnists said that he was creating a distraction for the team. Former Dallas Cowboys superstar Michael Irvin chose even harsher words. "To me, in my head, that's quitting," Irvin said on ESPN. "That's not retiring."

Barber countered the criticism with an eloquent response: "I have a lot of interests, and I've never wanted to be solely defined as a football player," he said, according to ESPN.com. "I wasn't that way in high school, I wasn't that way in college, and I won't compromise my ideals to be that way in the National Football League."

The abuse he took on the gridiron was another reason he was contemplating retirement. "When I get home from work, my kids come running at me," he said, as reported in *Sports Illustrated*. "They make me get on my knees, and we play tackle football. . . . I saw this video of O.J. Simpson once, and his kids came running at him and he couldn't even pick them up. So I can see that, if I play three or four more years, like everybody wants me to, that could be me. But when I'm 50 years old, and I'm having trouble just getting down the stairs, will they be cheering for me then?"

Sports Illustrated columnist Rick Reilly supported Barber's decision. Reilly stated that too many men had played too long in the NFL and lived to regret it. He told the story of 15-year veteran Jim Otto, who had endured 59 operations, including 48 on his knees. Reilly wrote, "His ankle looks like a science project. He's got rods up and down his spine. Arthritis in his feet and neck tortures him. He is 68."

THE MILLION-DOLLAR GIFT

In Week 4 of the 2006 NFL season, Tiki and Ronde Barber's teams both happened to have a bye. Instead of loafing around the house all weekend, the twin brothers traveled to their college alma mater, dressed in suits that matched their school colors, and gave the university twin checks of $500,000.

The Barbers' gift was announced during a dinner that launched the University of Virginia's $3 billion fund-raising campaign. Tiki and Ronde not only donated $1 million, but they also served as emcees for the evening.

"We've both done pretty well as NFL players and, as a result, have made a great living," Tiki said. "A lot of that is a result of being here at the university, not only being mentored and guided as football players but guided as people. The meaning of philanthropy is being able to make a difference to those who helped push you up."

Thirteen years earlier, Virginia gave the Barbers full-ride athletic scholarships. After graduation, Tiki showed his gratitude by serving on the Young Alumni Council. He also founded a program that encouraged young alumni to start a tradition of giving to the university. It was named MY-D-CAV (My Yearly Dollars Count at Virginia).

The Barbers' $1 million gift counted for a whole lot. Some of the money was given to the McIntire School of Commerce, from which Tiki and Ronde had received their undergraduate degrees. The money also went to the Young Alumni Council, the Virginia Athletics Foundation, the University of Virginia Children's Hospital, and a university scholarship fund that benefited African-American students. Half of the $1 million was issued in the form of a challenge to encourage young Virginia alumni to contribute to the fund-raising campaign.

Craig Littlepage, the school's athletic director, was among the many who lavished praise on the young philanthropists. According to a Giants press release, he called the brothers "great models for all alumni and all former student athletes," adding: "The generosity they demonstrate through this gift clearly shows how special Ronde and Tiki are."

A SPRINT TO THE FINISH

For the last 11 games of the 2006 season, Barber was determined to prove that he wasn't a "quitter." In the first game after his announcement, he rushed for 114 yards in New York's 36-22 win over Dallas—a Monday night game on ESPN that happened to be the most watched cable program in history (16,028,000 viewers). After Barber's 68- and 115-yard efforts against Tampa Bay and Houston, the Giants improved to 6–2. Against the vaunted Chicago Bears defense on Sunday night, Barber romped for 141 yards on just 19 carries. Unfortunately, the game marked the beginning of a tailspin that saw the Giants drop to 7–8. Over the abysmal 1–6 stretch, Barber gutted out an average of 85 yards per game.

In Week 14, Barber became the first running back in the 82-year history of the Giants to rush for 10,000 yards. He also became just the third NFL player to amass 10,000 rushing yards and 5,000 receiving yards. Previously, only Marshall Faulk and Marcus Allen had achieved the feat.

Despite their 7–8 record in 2006, the Giants would make the playoffs if they won their last game. Emotions ran high in the days preceding the Giants-Redskins matchup. Many were

(continues on page 98)

GIANT ACCOMPLISHMENTS

With his powerful build, quick moves, and terrific hands, Tiki Barber gained yards in every way imaginable. He not only shattered numerous team records, but he also achieved feats that few NFL players had ever accomplished. This is his legacy:

NEW YORK GIANTS TEAM RECORDS

Career
- Most rushing yards: 10,449
- Most rushing attempts: 2,217
- Most rushing touchdowns: 55
- Highest yards-per-carry average: 4.7
- Most 1,000-yard rushing seasons: 6
- Most total yards: 17,359

Season
- Most rushing yards: 1,860 (2005)
- Most rushing attempts: 357 (2005)
- Most 100-yard games: 9 (2004)
- Most 200-yard games: 3 (2005)
- Most total yards: 2,390 (2005)

Game
- Most rushing yards: 234 (December 30, 2006, vs. Washington)
- Longest touchdown run: 95 yards (December 31, 2005, vs. Oakland)
- Most total yards: 276; 203 rushing, 73 receiving (December 28, 2002, vs. Philadelphia)

NFL ACHIEVEMENTS

- Became the twenty-first player in NFL history to amass 10,000 career rushing yards.
- Joined Marshall Faulk and Marcus Allen as the only NFL players to eclipse 10,000 yards rushing and 5,000 yards receiving.
- Became the fourth NFL player to produce four seasons of 2,000 total yards.
- Became the tenth NFL player to amass 400 career receptions and 10,000 yards rushing.
- Became the first player in NFL history to accumulate 1,800 yards rushing and 500 yards receiving in the same season (2005).
- Became the third NFL player with three 200-yard rushing games in one season (2005).
- Exceeded 100 yards rushing in a game 38 times.
- Produced five 200-yard rushing games in his career.
- Joined Walter Payton (Chicago Bears) and James Wilder (Tampa Bay Buccaneers) as the only NFL players to reign as their team's career leader in both rushing yards and receptions. (In 2007, Amani Toomer eclipsed Barber's career reception mark of 586.)
- Set an NFL record by leading his team in rushing for 80 consecutive games (2002 to 2006).
- Led the NFL in total yards from scrimmage in 2004 (2,096) and 2005 (2,390).
- Named to the Pro Bowl for the 2004, 2005, and 2006 seasons.

(continued from page 95)

demanding that the team fire head coach Tom Coughlin. The coach, meanwhile, had several heart-to-heart talks with his players during the week.

As for Barber, he faced the reality that this could be his last football game ever. "There are certain things that motivate you, push you," he said, according to ESPN.com. "It's partly because of the circumstances of this game, my last one. Most important, we had to win to keep playing."

On a cool, sunny day at Washington's FedEx Field, Tiki Barber delivered. In the second quarter, he broke a tackle and rambled 55 yards. Later in the quarter, he maintained his balance after being tripped up and scampered 15 yards for a touchdown.

Eli Manning was averaging less than four yards per passing attempt, but Barber's heroics helped New York put points on the board. With the Giants up 27-21 late in the fourth quarter, Tiki sealed the game with a 50-yard run. He cut to the left, cut to the right, broke a tackle, and sprinted to the end zone. New York prevailed 34-28 to clinch a playoff berth.

In his final regular-season game, Barber set the all-time single-game rushing record by a New York Giant. On 23 carries, he rushed for 234 yards and three touchdowns. He demolished the NFL record for most yards by a running back in his final regular-season game (165 by Cliff Battles in 1937).

"That's why he's Tiki Barber," said Giants linebacker Antonio Pierce after the game. "He plays with a lot of heart and determination. Today he put this team and this offense on his back and did everything he could for us to win."

Barber finished the season with 1,662 rushing yards. Only three backs in the NFL rushed for more: LaDainian Tomlinson of San Diego (1,815), Larry Johnson of Kansas City (1,789), and Frank Gore of San Francisco (1,695). But the biggest game of the year lay ahead, in the playoffs. New York would visit the 10–6 Philadelphia Eagles, champions of the NFC East.

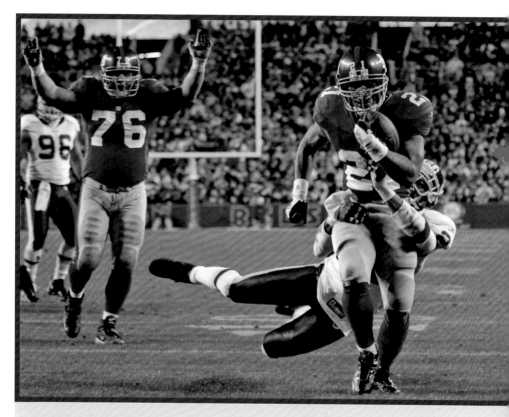

In his final regular-season game on December 30, 2006, Tiki Barber drags Redskins safety Sean Taylor into the end zone for a touchdown during the first half. Barber set a Giants single-game rushing record with 234 yards, and with a victory over Washington, New York made the playoffs.

A WARRIOR'S FINAL BATTLE

The Eagles, known for their bruising defense, had limited Barber to 126 yards rushing combined in their two meetings in 2006. Moreover, after the game, Barber would call Lincoln Financial Field "one of the hardest places I've ever played in." Nevertheless, the Giants star pounded away at the Eagles' defense. In the second quarter, he broke loose for 41 yards, setting up a Giants field goal.

Down 20-13, New York quarterback Eli Manning orchestrated a brilliant 80-yard drive to tie the score. Perhaps, Giants fans hoped, their team could accomplish the feat of the Steelers one year earlier. Pittsburgh had won three playoff games on the road and then triumphed in the Super Bowl. Along the way, running back Jerome Bettis had become a national hero by winning a championship in what he had announced would be his last season. Would Tiki Barber be the Jerome Bettis of the 2006 campaign?

Unfortunately for New Yorkers, the dream died in the closing seconds. Philadelphia's David Akers booted a 38-yard field goal as time expired for a 23-20 Eagles victory. Despite grinding out 137 yards, Barber's career ended with a painful loss. Afterward, Eagles star safety Brian Dawkins walked up to Barber and told him, "You're a warrior."

Barber's mother, Geraldine, had known that for years. After the game, she expressed pride and joy for her superstar son. "I'm very happy for him," she said in an article on ESPN.com. "I wasn't too emotional at the end, because I realize he's ready to begin another stage of his life. . . . It's time to turn the page, turn to the next chapter, like any good book."

Life's Next Chapter

While adorned in a floral lei, Tiki Barber admired the skyline of Waikiki, Hawaii. Some players receive a gold watch upon retirement. Barber was treated to a Pro Bowl game in Honolulu in February 2007—with all expenses paid. "I got off the plane. Got a lei. Got a kiss. And I knew the next 10 days of my life would be beautiful," he said, as reported in the *New York Post*.

Football fans certainly did not consider the young retiree a "quitter," as some in the media had suggested. In fan balloting for the Pro Bowl, Barber finished fourth, behind superstars Peyton Manning, LaDainian Tomlinson, and Drew Brees. Before the game, Barber talked about his recent retirement. He explained how football was a young man's game. It was for those who could play on Sunday and feel refreshed on Tuesday, he said. In his final season, Barber felt awful on Tuesdays and did not get rejuvenated until the end of each week. For that reason and others, Barber had no regrets about hanging up his cleats for good.

"I had a great career, and it ended on my terms," he said in the *New York Post.* "I wasn't carried off the field on a stretcher. I didn't sustain a major injury that prevented me from doing what I love to do. Now I get to do something else."

On February 12, two days after the Pro Bowl, Barber submitted his retirement papers to the NFL Players Association. He had no trouble finding a new job, as Fox, ABC/ESPN, and NBC bid for his services. Barber signed with NBC in order to pursue one of his lifelong ambitions. "My dream has always been to be on the *Today* show," he told the press.

He would indeed work as a correspondent on *Today*, the highest-rated morning news show on television. In addition, he would serve as a commentator for NBC's *Football Night in America.*

On February 13, NBC staged a news conference to show off its new employee. Barber looked sharp in his pinstriped suit, with a stylish handkerchief in his suit-jacket pocket. Barber stated that he was interested in doing stories on health and technology. NBC Universal CEO Jeff Zucker was just glad he was on board. "Tiki Barber is one of those rare personalities who appeals to virtually every audience imaginable," Zucker said.

NBC News President Steve Capus added that Barber was "just going to light up the screen." Capus also added a corny "twins" joke. "On those days when you're not feeling well," Capus quipped, "we'll just call Tampa Bay and get your brother."

However, what was supposed to be a feel-good press conference digressed into something more disturbing. Barber stated that Giants coach Tom Coughlin had pushed him too hard in practice.

Tiki Barber signs autographs in February 2007 at the Ihilani Resort in Kapolei, Hawaii, before an NFC team practice for the Pro Bowl. Two days after the Pro Bowl, Barber submitted his official retirement papers to the NFL Players Association.

"There'd be days where I couldn't move on Tuesday or Wednesday at practice, and he'd get mad at me for going half-speed," Barber said. "And I told him, 'Coach, I can't do it. I'm going to be out here, I'm never going to miss a practice, but I can't give you what you want all the time.' And he understood."

Barber knew his words would make the next morning's headlines, but he felt a need to vent his feelings. "We were in full pads for 17 weeks," he continued, "and with the amount of injuries that we had, it just takes a toll on you. You just physically don't want to be out there when your body feels the way you do in full pads. And while it probably doesn't have a really detrimental effect on how you practice or how you play, it does on your mind. And if you lose your mind in this game, you lose a lot. And that's something that [Coughlin] has to realize. And I think he does [now]."

After getting that off his chest, Barber was ready to begin his exciting new career.

TODAY'S ROOKIE

Just two months after signing with *Today,* Barber was scheduled to make his premiere on the show. Barber treated those weeks like a football training camp. He spent long hours at the

TODAY

Hundreds of television shows fill the airwaves, but only a few are national institutions—with *Today* near the top of the list. When the show premiered on NBC on January 14, 1952, it changed Americans' morning routines. No longer would they get their news solely from the local newspaper. *Today* host Dave Garroway told the *national* story, with audio news streaming into the New York studio from Washington, London, and Germany.

Today informed and entertained with a mix of hard news, interviews, lifestyle features, and funny gimmicks. Chimpanzee J. Fred Muggs, in his silly little outfits, served as the show's mascot. The show spawned imitation morning programs on ABC and CBS, but *Today* has always been the king. Such legendary newscasters as John Chancellor, Hugh Downs, Barbara Walters, Tom Brokaw, Bryant Gumbel, and Katie Couric have hosted the show.

Broadcasting from Rockefeller Center in New York, *Today* has been the highest-rated morning news and talk show in the United States since 1995. Currently, Matt Lauer and Meredith Vieira co-host *Today's* first two hours, teaming with hilarious

NBC offices figuring out the business. He learned about script-writing and tape editing, and he practiced reading off a Tele-PrompTer. He even learned how to apply his own makeup.

Barber discovered that certain details had to be addressed—subtleties that the television audience did not realize. One humorous issue had to do with his noggin. "I have issues with my bald head and how they have to light me," he told the *New York Daily News*. "The light has to be at my shoulders, otherwise I get a halo effect."

weatherman Al Roker. In September 2007, the show expanded from three hours to four (7:00 A.M. to 11:00 A.M.), providing more opportunities for the new guy, Tiki Barber.

The *Today* show refers to Barber as a "correspondent." Like media celebrities Joe Garagiola and Gene Shalit before him, Barber makes studio appearances, conducts interviews, and reports on a wide range of topics.

It is very possible that Barber will spend many years with *Today*. First of all, he is a man of loyalty, as evidenced by his devotion to his family, his alma mater, and the Giants, for whom he played his entire career. Moreover, unlike with other television programs, newscasters tend to stick with *Today*. Hosts Bryant Gumbel, Matt Lauer, Jane Pauley, and Katie Couric lasted at least 13 years each with the show. Moreover, correspondents Edwin Newman (1952–1984) and Gene Shalit (1973–present) hung around for decades.

After 10 years in the NFL and now a fixture on NBC, Barber could wind up spending most of his life on television. As a shy kid growing up, he never would have believed it.

Before his scheduled premiere on *Today,* Barber sat down for an interview with Jen Brown of TODAYshow.com. He talked about challenges. "My entire career, from the time I was a rookie to 10 years later, my goal was to constantly reinvent myself, to find whatever my fault was or whatever I was deficient in and reinvent myself into something powerful," Barber said. "It got to the point where I couldn't reinvent myself anymore. . . . When you hit the top of your profession, what do you aspire to?"

Barber told Brown that he eventually wanted to talk news and politics on the NBC airwaves. But that was the domain of the top reporters and analysts. "I understand there's a process to get there," he said. "I'm starting at the bottom again."

The "bottom" began on April 16, 2007—one of the darkest days for America in the twenty-first century.

Barber's first piece for *Today* was supposed to air on that fateful Monday morning. He had interviewed Marcus Buckingham, a highly successful motivational speaker. But NBC shelved that feel-good piece because of the tragedy that was unfolding in Blacksburg, Virginia. Seung-Hui Cho, a deeply disturbed Virginia Tech student, went on a shooting rampage. He killed 32 people, mostly students, and wounded many others before taking his own life.

Soon after the massacre began, Elena Nachmanoff, vice president of talent for NBC News, asked Barber if he wanted to go to Blacksburg to help cover the story. Barber felt compelled to say yes. He had grown up in Roanoke, only 40 miles (64 kilometers) north of the college town, and both of his parents had attended the school. For the first time in years, he returned to Blacksburg.

"Covering such a major tragic event," Barber wrote on his *Today* show blog, "was exciting and terrifying, tragically sad and eye-opening." Barber walked around campus interviewing shaken students. The following day, he did a story about the Blacksburg community and how it was impacted by the horrific

On the *Today* show set, Tiki Barber talks with hosts Meredith Vieira and Matt Lauer on April 16, 2007—Barber's first day as a national correspondent with the show. That morning, a gunman killed 32 people at Virginia Tech, and NBC sent Barber to Blacksburg, Virginia, as part of its coverage of the massacre.

events. Barber wrote: "I left Blacksburg having vast sorrow inside for too many young lives lost prematurely. I also came to understand the value of a story, and the urgency and challenge it takes to bring it to the public."

SOUTH AFRICAN ADVENTURES

Covering such a major news event was unheard of for a novice network-news reporter. But his baptism by fire continued. Just days after the Virginia Tech story, Barber was dispatched halfway around the world to report on another serious issue.

Matt Lauer, the lead anchorman for *Today*, began his annual segment called "Where in the World Is Matt Lauer?" For years, Barber had enjoyed watching Lauer's reports from around the globe. Now he had a chance to go with him, accompanying Lauer to South Africa. One of his assignments: report on shantytowns in the once racially segregated country.

From 1948 to the early 1990s, South Africa operated under the system of apartheid. To maintain its power, the country's white population instituted laws that deliberately oppressed the black population—even though most South Africans were black. Blacks were forced to live on the edge of society and in miserable conditions.

Despite the abolition of apartheid, Barber reported that great numbers of black South Africans still lived in crowded, dismal shantytowns. He noted that economic conditions are gradually improving for blacks, but that true equality is a long, long way away.

Barber's trip to South Africa was not without its problems. Sean Reis, a producer for *Today*, recounted how Barber's flight to that country was delayed 12 hours—and that his luggage was lost. While Barber was still en route, Reis had to go out and buy him clothes. These included shirts, socks, shoes, and underwear. "It's a rather odd experience shopping for another man," Reis wrote in his blog.

The hardest part was finding proper pants. Despite a small waist (32 inches), Barber had tree-trunk-size thighs. But Reis bought all his clothes, prompting thank-yous and a good dose of teasing from Barber.

It was no joke, however, when Barber arrived at South Africa's Shark Alley to swim with the great white shark. The largest predator fish in the world, the great white can shred a man to pieces in seconds. But Brian McFarland, Barber's experienced guide, explained on the air that the great white was not a "monster" but a "beautiful, graceful animal" that did "not want to touch, hurt, or harm you at all."

"Completely safe?" Barber asked before jumping in with the sharks.

"Absolutely," McFarland said. "But never say never."

Barber smiled (sort of) and soon donned a wet suit. Under McFarland's watchful eye, Barber entered a cage attached to their boat. Using a severed tuna head as bait, the group soon attracted a great white. At one point, the shark thrashed wildly against the cage. Though he was nervous at first, Barber's thoughts turned to fascination and respect for the animal's "majesty and grace." At one point, he even reached out of the cage to try to touch the beautiful beast. Afterward, Lauer couldn't believe what Barber had done. "That's ridiculous!" Lauer teased. Barber could only laugh.

"Two weeks on the job," Barber wrote in his blog, "and I'm on the ground (or in the water) running . . . and loving every minute of it."

CHARITY AND CONTROVERSY

On May 10, 2007, Barber continued his charitable work by hosting "Tiki Rocks the Square for Children's Miracle Network." The VIP event benefited a charity that was dedicated to saving and improving the lives of children. The organization raised funds for children's hospitals throughout North America. Superstar rocker Jon Bon Jovi, a friend of Barber's, provided entertainment. "These children have had a tremendous impact on me," Barber was quoted as saying on Starpulse.com, "and it's a great feeling knowing that I can help make a difference in their lives as well."

Barber continued to light up New York by co-hosting the *Macy's Fourth of July Fireworks Spectacular*. Barber tried his best to act natural and have a good time. The result was a ratings success, as NBC beat out its rival networks during that 9:00 to 10:00 P.M. time slot.

Despite delving into news and entertainment, Barber could not escape the sports pages. In July, Giants quarterback Eli Manning took a jab at Barber when he told the *New York Daily News:* "We're excited by the players that we have who wanted to return for this season, and who wanted to be a part of the Giants and play."

The media pounced on the story, stating that Manning and the Giants resented that Barber had retired—or quit. Manning and Barber continued to make national headlines with their war of words. As a halftime analyst for NBC's *Sunday Night Football,* Barber said that Manning was "uncomfortable" when it came to motivating teammates. Barber added, "Sometimes it was almost comical the way he would say things."

Manning retaliated by telling reporters: "I could have questioned his leadership skills last year—calling out the coach, retiring in the middle of the season—that he'd lost the heart."

Tiki, along with Ronde, further criticized Manning on their Sirius radio show, *The Barber Shop.* Tiki opined that former Giants quarterback Kerry Collins was the "true" leader of the team and that the Giants never should have let him go. Superstar quarterback Peyton Manning joined the fray by vigorously defending his younger brother.

CHALLENGES AHEAD

Barber's harsh criticism raised a lot of ethical questions. Many NFL players believed that he should not have aired his former team's "dirty laundry" on the airwaves. Such personal matters, they believed, should have remained in the locker room. Another question: Was Barber being a good critical analyst by discussing Manning's "flaws"? Or did he deliver a personal, retaliatory attack against Manning because the quarterback had implied that he was a quitter? If the latter were true, was that the mark of a good journalist?

As long as he stays in journalism, Barber will continuously have to weigh what's right and what's wrong. Being a commentator on television is particularly challenging. Networks desperately desire high ratings, which equal big money. This means that they want football analysts like Barber to make bold statements, which may compromise good journalism.

During halftime of the Virginia-Virginia Tech game on November 24, 2007, the University of Virginia retired Tiki Barber's jersey. Barber attended the game with his two sons, A.J. *(right)* and Chason. With his family at his side, Barber is sure to meet whatever endeavors he decides to take on.

Barber faced even greater challenges in the fall of 2007. In addition to his duties on *Football Night in America,* he took on a larger role with *Today* because the show expanded by a full hour. In September, the Associated Press asked if Barber was a true journalist. "In some ways it's a loose term but, yes, I think I am," Barber responded. "I think a journalist is someone who tells stories, and I do it in my own way and with my own voice."

Barber had played more than 20 years of football before he mastered his craft. He and those closest to him realize that his new career will be just as challenging. "Given a little bit of time, he'll earn his stripes," Matt Lauer told the Associated Press. "Does he come with those stripes? No. But a lot of us didn't."

Even if Tiki gets a swelled head, Ronde will be there to offer perspective. In fact, Ronde appears to be Tiki's harshest critic. "To this day—and he's only been [on *Today*] since April—I have not seen him nail anything yet that I would give him credit for," Ronde told AP in the late summer of 2007. "Even if he did, I probably wouldn't tell him. I don't want to be the guy that's telling him that he's made it, because then you lose interest and I don't want him to do that."

Certainly, Tiki is not one to rest on his laurels. All his life, he has taken on great challenges and emerged victorious. With his family at his side, he excelled in the classroom, pushed himself to his physical limits, overcame his fumbling woes, and developed into a dominating football star.

All the while, he has shown that true success isn't measured in winning percentage or yards per carry. It is reflected in human decency and in love for family and friends. A role model for young and old, Barber has improved his mind, expanded his horizons, and given generously to those less fortunate. And he's done it all, of course, with a smile.

STATISTICS

TIKI BARBER
Position: Running back

FULL NAME:
Atiim Kiambu Barber
BORN: **April 7, 1975,
Blacksburg, Virginia**
HEIGHT: **5'10"**

WEIGHT: **205 lbs.**
COLLEGE: **University
of Virginia**
TEAM: **New York Giants
(1997–2006)**

YEAR	TEAM	G	ATT	YARDS	Y/C	TD	REC	YARDS	Y/R	TD
1997	NYG	12	136	511	3.8	3	34	299	8.8	1
1998	NYG	16	52	166	3.2	0	42	348	8.3	3
1999	NYG	16	62	258	4.2	0	66	609	9.2	2
2000	NYG	16	213	1,006	4.7	8	70	719	10.3	1
2001	NYG	14	166	865	5.2	4	72	577	8.0	0
2002	NYG	16	304	1,387	4.6	11	69	597	8.7	0
2003	NYG	16	278	1,216	4.4	2	69	461	6.7	1
2004	NYG	16	322	1,518	4.7	13	52	578	11.1	2
2005	NYG	16	357	1,860	5.2	9	54	530	9.8	2
2006	NYG	16	327	1,662	5.1	5	58	465	8.0	0
TOTALS		**154**	**2,217**	**10,449**	**4.7**	**55**	**586**	**5,183**	**8.8**	**12**

CHRONOLOGY

1975   April 7 Born along with identical twin brother, Ronde, in Blacksburg, Virginia.

1989–1993   Amasses awards in football and track at Cave Spring High School in Roanoke, Virginia; graduates as valedictorian.

1993–1994   Excels in track and the classroom, but sees little playing time on the football field, during his first two years at the University of Virginia.

1995   November 2 Racks up 301 total yards as Virginia upsets Florida State 33-28.
Rushes for 1,397 yards, a season record at Virginia.

TIMELINE

1975
Born on April 7 with identical twin brother, Ronde, in Blacksburg, Virginia

1997
Drafted in the second round by the New York Giants

1999
Marries Virginia "Ginny" Joy Cha

1975   **2000**

1995
Rushes for 1,397 yards, a season record at the University of Virginia

2000
Finishes his breakout season with a Giants-record 2,085 all-purpose yards

1997   Drafted in the second round (thirty-sixth overall) by the New York Giants; Ronde is selected in the third round by the Tampa Bay Buccaneers.

1997–1999   Averages just 312 yards rushing (but 419 reception yards) per season during his first three NFL seasons.

1999   **February** Adopts his grueling hill-climbing routine. **May 15** Marries Virginia "Ginny" Joy Cha.

2000   Finishes his breakout season with 1,006 yards rushing and a Giants-record 2,085 all-purpose yards; the team goes 12-4.

2001   **January 14** Contributes to the Giants' 41-0 romp over Minnesota in the NFC Championship Game.

2002
Amasses a team-record 276 total yards in game against Philadelphia

2006
Rushes for a Giants-record 234 yards in regular-season finale

2001

2007

2001
Rushes for 49 yards in the Super Bowl

2005
Breaks the Giants' season and career rushing records on January 2

2007
Plays in final game, a playoff loss to Philadelphia; joins *Today* show as a correspondent

TIKI BARBER

January 28 Rushes for 49 yards in the Super Bowl, which New York drops to Baltimore 34-7.
Leads the Giants in rushing with 865 yards during the 2001 season.

2002   **July 8** Becomes a father, as Ginny gives birth to Atiim Kiambu, Jr.
November 24 Begins a streak of four games with rushes of 40 yards or more (an NFL record).
December 28 Rushes for 203 yards, with a team-record 276 total yards, against Philadelphia.

2003   Rushes for 1,216 yards during the season, with 461 receiving yards.

2004   **March 18** Becomes a father for a second time, as son Chason is born.
Spring Works with his coaches on adopting a new grip (to cure his fumbling problems); also begins serious weight training.
May 15 Delivers a valedictory address at the University of Virginia.

2005   **January 2** Breaks the Giants' season and career rushing records, and scores the winning touchdown with 11 seconds left, against Dallas.
February 13 Plays in his first of three straight Pro Bowls.
October 30 Honors Giants owner Wellington Mara, who died five days earlier, by rushing for 206 yards in a rout of Washington.
December 31 Rips off a 95-yard run against Oakland, the longest in Giants history.
Finishes the season with 1,860 rushing yards and 2,390 all-purpose yards (second most in NFL history).

2006   **September 30** Along with Ronde, donates $1 million to
the University of Virginia.
December 10 Becomes the twenty-first NFL player to
rush for 10,000 yards in his career.
Finishes the season with 1,662 yards rushing, including
a Giants-record 234 yards in the finale to help New
York make the playoffs.

2007   **January 7** Rushes for 137 yards in a wild-card game loss
to Philadelphia—his last NFL game.
February 13 Joins NBC as a *Today* show correspondent
and *Sunday Night Football* commentator.
April 16 Reports on the shooting massacre at Virginia
Tech University for the *Today* show.
September His memoir, *Tiki,* is published by Simon &
Schuster.

GLOSSARY

all-purpose yards   The sum of all yards gained by a player who is in possession of the ball during a play. These yards include rushing and receiving yards gained on offense, yards gained on returns of interceptions and fumbles, and yards gained on kickoff and punt returns.

box   The area on the defensive side of the ball directly opposite the offensive linemen and about five yards deep; having eight players in the box means bringing in a defensive back to help stop the offensive team's running game.

carry   The act of running with the ball.

center   A player position on offense. The center snaps the ball.

defensive back   A cornerback or safety position on the defensive team; commonly defends against wide receivers on passing plays. Generally there are four defensive backs playing at a time.

draft   The selection of collegiate players for entrance into the National Football League. Typically, the team with the worst record in the previous season picks first in the draft.

draw play   A play in which the quarterback drops back as if to pass but then hands the ball off to the running back or runs with it himself.

end zone   The area between the end line and the goal line, bounded by the sidelines.

extra point   After a touchdown, the scoring team is allowed to add another point by kicking the football through the uprights of the goalpost.

field goal   A scoring play of three points made by kicking the ball through the goalposts in the opponent's end zone.

fullback   A player position on offense. In modern formations this position may be varied, and this player has more blocking responsibilities in comparison to the halfback or the tailback.

fumble   When any offensive player loses possession of the ball before the play is blown dead.

hamstring   Any of three muscles at the back of the thigh that function to flex and rotate the leg and extend the thigh.

handoff   The act of giving the ball to another player; generally occurs when the quarterback hands the ball to a running back, but it can take place between any two teammates.

Heisman Trophy   An award presented annually to the most outstanding player in Division I-A college football.

holding   A penalty in which one player keeps another from advancing by grabbing him and holding him back. Offensive holding is a 10-yard penalty, and the down is repeated. Defensive holding results in a five-yard penalty and an automatic first down.

interception   A pass that is caught by a defensive player, giving his team the ball.

kickoff   A kick that puts the ball into play at the start of the first and third quarters and after every touchdown and field goal.

kick returner   A player on the receiving team who specializes in fielding kickoffs and running them back.

ligament   A sheet or band of tough, fibrous tissue that connects bones or cartilage at a joint or that holds an organ of the body in place.

linebacker   A player position on defense. Linebackers typically play one to six yards behind the defensive linemen. Most defenses use either three or four linebackers.

misdirection play   A type of offensive play that seems to head in one direction but then goes in another. For example, such a play may involve faking to one back who is going one way and giving the ball to another back going the other way.

National Football Conference (NFC)   One of the two conferences in the National Football League (NFL). The NFC was established after the NFL merged with the American Football League (AFL) in 1970.

option   A type of play in which the quarterback has the option to hand off the ball, keep it himself, or laterally pass it to one or more backs.

pass interference   Illegally hindering another player's chances of catching a forward pass.

penalty   Punishment for an infraction of the rules.

placekicker   The player who kicks the ball on kickoffs, field-goal attempts, and extra-point attempts.

pocket   The area of protection given to a quarterback by his offensive line when he drops back to pass.

Pro Bowl   The all-star game of the NFL, played a week after the Super Bowl. Players are voted to the Pro Bowl by coaches, fellow players, and fans. Each group's ballots count for one-third of the vote.

punt   A kick in which the ball is dropped and kicked before it hits the ground. A punt usually occurs on fourth down and is used to push the opposing team as far back as possible before it takes possession of the ball.

quarterback   The offensive player who receives the ball from the center at the start of each play. The quarterback will hand off the ball, pass the ball, or run it himself.

rollout pass   When the quarterback moves left or right out of the pocket before passing the ball.

rookie   A player in his first year as a professional.

running back   An offensive player who runs with the football; also known as a tailback, halfback, or fullback.

rush   A running play; also, an attempt to tackle or hurry a player before he can make a pass or kick the ball.

safety   A defensive player who lines up in the secondary but often deeper than the cornerbacks.

screen play   A forward pass to a receiver at or behind the line of scrimmage who is protected by a screen of blockers.

tackle   The act of forcing a ball carrier to the ground; also, a player position on the offensive or defensive line.

touchdown   A play worth six points in which any part of the ball while legally in the possession of a player crosses the plane of the opponent's goal line. A touchdown allows the team a chance for one extra point by kicking the ball or a two-point conversion by running or passing the ball into the end zone.

turnover   A loss of possession of the ball by either a fumble or an interception.

two-point conversion   A scoring play immediately after a touchdown during which a team can add two points to the score instead of kicking for just one point. In a two-point conversion, the scoring team has one play to run or pass the ball into the end zone from the opponent's 3-yard line in college football and 2-yard line in the NFL.

wide receiver   A player position on offense. He is split wide (usually about 10 yards) from the formation and plays on the line of scrimmage as a split end or one yard off as a flanker.

wild card   The two playoff spots given to the two nondivision-winning teams that have the best records in the conference.

yard   One yard of linear distance in the direction of one of the two goals. A field is 100 yards. Typically, a team is required to advance at least 10 yards in order to get a new set of downs.

BIBLIOGRAPHY

BOOKS

Barber, Tiki and Gil Reavill. *Tiki: My Life in the Game and Beyond.* New York: Simon & Schuster, 2007.

MAGAZINES

Altobelli, Lisa. "The Beat." *Sports Illustrated*, May 2, 2005.

Amsden, David. "Tiki Barber: The Exit Interview." *New York*, January 15, 2007.

Best, Neil. "Offseason Project." *Sporting News*, June 17, 2005.

"A Football Giant." *Current Events*, February 5, 2007.

Greenfeld, Karl Taro. "Media Giant?" *Sports Illustrated*, December 18, 2006.

"Having a Ball." *People Weekly*, January 29, 2001.

Kennedy, Kostya. "The Third Barber." *Sports Illustrated*, December 12, 2005.

King, Peter. "Trading E-Mail with . . . Giants Multipurpose Running Back Tiki Barber." *Sports Illustrated*, October 6, 2003.

McGrath, Ben. "Walking Away." *The New Yorker*, January 29, 2007.

Pompei, Dan. "Thunder and Lightning Become a Flammable Mix." *Sporting News*, September 25, 2000.

"Q & A Tiki Barber." *Sports Illustrated*, April 11, 2005.

Reilly, Rick. "A Barber Who Won't Cut It Close." *Sports Illustrated*, November 13, 2006.

Rosenthal, Jim. "Sibling Rivalry?" *Muscle & Fitness*, October 2003.

"Tackling Tooth Decay." *Jet*, April 3, 2006.

"Tiki Barber." *Sports Illustrated*, December 13, 2004.

Wilner, Barry. "The Power of One." *Football Digest*, January 2001.

Yorio, Kara. "More Than Holding His Own." *Sporting News*, October 25, 2004.

NEWSPAPERS

Lipke, David. "They've Got the Look." *Daily News Record*, April 8, 2002.

Vehorn, Frank. "The Barbers of C'Ville." *The Virginian-Pilot*, November 2, 1995.

ONLINE ARTICLES

Barber, Tiki. "Mr. Tiki Barber, Valedictory Address." Office of Major Events, May 15, 2004. Available online at *http://www.virginia.edu/majorevents/speeches/04valspeech.html*.

Bauder, David. "Tiki Barber Joins NBC to Work at *Today*." *The Washington Post*, February 13, 2007. Available online at *http://www.washingtonpost.com/wp-dyn/content/article/2007/02/13/AR2007021300721.html*.

Branch, John. "After a Tete-a-Tete, Barber Tones It Down." *The New York Times*, January 10, 2006. Available online at *http://www.nytimes.com/2006/01/10/sports/football/10giants.html?ex=1188619200&en=0bc85916d7d568f4&ei=5070*.

Brown, Jen. "Tiki Barber Makes 'Giant' Debut on *Today*." MSNBC, April 16, 2007. Available online at *http://www.msnbc.msn.com/id/18123547*.

"College Flashback." *U.S. News & World Report*, no date. Available online at *http://www.usnews.com/usnews/edu/college/student-center/flashback/flashback_090805_brief.php*.

Eisen, Michael. "Giants Over Eagles in OT, 10-7." Official Site of the New York Giants, December 28, 2002. Available online at *http://www.giants.com/news/eisen/story.asp?story_id=273*.

———. "Giants Fall to Cowboys, 35-32." Official Site of the New York Giants, September 15, 2003. Available online at *http://www.giants.com/news/eisen/story.asp?story_id=476*.

———. "Giants Fall to Cowboys, 19-3." Official Site of the New York Giants, December 21, 2003. Available online at *http://www.giants.com/news/eisen/story.asp?story_id=404.*

———. "Players, Fans Say Goodbye to Fassel." Official Site of the New York Giants, December 28, 2003. Available online at *http://www.giants.com/news/eisen/story.asp?story_id=242.*

———. "Giants Fall to Eagles, 31-17." Official Site of the New York Giants, September 12, 2004. Available online at *http://www.giants.com/news/eisen/story.asp?story_id=1520.*

———. "Giants Over Cowboys, 28-24." Official Site of the New York Giants, January 2, 2005. Available online at *http://www.giants.com/news/eisen/story.asp?story_id=4691.*

———. "Giants to Mark 9/11 Anniversary with Special Game-day Ceremonies." Official Site of the New York Giants, September 7, 2005. Available online at *http://www.giants.com/news/eisen/story.asp?story_id=8416.*

Finkel, Jon. "Giant Among Men." *Men's Fitness,* November 2003. Available online at *http://findarticles.com/p/articles/mi_m1608/is_11_19/ai_110809239.*

Foeman, Lisa R. "A Mother's Dynamic Duo." MOSAEC, December 2006. Available online at *http://www.mosaec.com/mosaec/sports/sports_barber.htm.*

"Giants Outrun Chiefs 27-17." National Football League, December 17, 2005. Available online at *http://www.nfl.com/gamecenter/recap;jsessionid=DBD6DB2A8B51CA8F9595C82EC87EEC8C?game_id=28734&displayPage=tab_recap&season=2005&week=REG15.*

Littlejohn, Janice Rhoshalle. "Former NFL Star Tiki Barber Seriously Pursuing New Goal: A Journalism Career." September 4, 2007, Macleans. Available online at *http://www.macleans.ca/article.jsp?content=e090433A.*

Pedulla, Tom. "Giants Pay Tribute to Mara By Whitewashing Redskins." *USA Today,* October 30, 2005. Available online at *http://www.usatoday.com/sports/football/games/2005-10-30-giants-redskins_x.htm.*

———. "Giants' Manning Barks Back at Barber." *USA Today,* August 21, 2007. Available online at *http://www.usatoday.com/sports/football/nfl/giants/2007-08-21-tiki-eli_N.htm.*

"Tiki and Ronde Barber Make $1 Million Gift to U.Va." Official Site of the New York Giants, October 2, 2006. Available online at *http://www.giants.com/news/press_releases/story.asp?story_id=19725.*

"Tiki Barber, Jon Bon Jovi Rock Times Square For Children's Miracle Network." Starpulse, May 9, 2007. Available online at *http://www.starpulse.com/news/index.php/2007/05/09/tiki_barber_jon_bon_jovi_rock_times_squa.*

Vacchiano, Ralph. "Live for *Today." New York Daily News,* April 1, 2007. Available online at *http://www.nydailynews.com/entertainment/tv/2007/04/01/2007-04-01_live_for_today-1.html.*

Weisman, Larry. "Panthers Whitewash Giants 23-0, Will Face Bears Next." *USA Today,* January 8, 2006. Available online at *http://www.usatoday.com/sports/football/games/2006-01-08-panthers-giants_x.htm.*

WEB SITES

CBS Sports
http://cbs.sportsline.com

ESPN
http://espn.go.com

Official Site of the National Football League
http://www.nfl.com

Official Site of the New York Giants

http://www.giants.com

Pro Football Reference

http://www.pro-football-reference.com

FURTHER READING

BOOKS

Bass, Tom. *Youth Football Skills and Drills.* New York: McGraw-Hill, 2005.

Benson, Michael. *The Good, the Bad, & the Ugly: Heart-Pounding, Jaw-Dropping, and Gut-Wrenching Moments in New York Giants History.* Chicago: Triumph Books, 2007.

Director, Roger. *I Dream in Blue: Life, Death, and the New York Giants.* New York: HarperCollins, 2007.

Eisen, Michael. *Stadium Stories: New York Giants.* Guilford, Conn.: Globe Pequot, 2005.

Long, Howie and John Czarnecki. *Football for Dummies.* New York: John Wiley and Sons, 2007.

Needham, Tom. *Tiki Barber: All-Pro On and Off the Field.* Berkeley Heights, N.J.: Enslow Publishers, 2007.

Palmer, Ken and Tiki Barber. *Game of My Life: New York Giants.* Champaign, Ill.: Sports Publishing, LLC, 2007.

Palmer, Pete, et al. *The ESPN Pro Football Encyclopedia.* New York: Sterling Publishing, 2007.

Schwartz, Paul. *Tales from the New York Giants Sideline.* Champaign, Ill.: Sports Publishing, LLC, 2007.

2007 NFL Record & Fact Book. New York: National Football League, 2007.

Whittingham, Richard. *What Giants They Were.* Chicago: Triumph Books, 2001.

_____. *Illustrated History of the New York Giants.* Chicago: Triumph Books, 2005.

WEB SITES

Fox Sports on MSN
http://msn.foxsports.com/nfl

NFL: Sunday Night Football

http://www.snfonnbc.com

SI.com—NFL

http://sportsillustrated.cnn.com/football/nfl

Sporting News

http://www.sportingnews.com/nfl

University of Virginia Cavaliers Official Athletic Site

http://www.virginiasports.com

PICTURE CREDITS

INDEX

ABOUT THE AUTHOR

DAVID ARETHA has written more than 30 books for young readers, including books on the Dallas Cowboys and the Pittsburgh Steelers. He has also edited dozens of sports and history books, including *Football Legends of All Time* and *Michigan Football: Yesterday & Today.*